UNAPOLOGETICALLY FREE:

Deliverance and Freedom Through the Spirit-Filled Life

TERESA G. LUSK

Teresa G. Lusk

CONTENTS

Printed in the United States of America

First Printing, 2019

ISBN 978-0692123034

Teresa G. Lusk

PO BOX 550 N Central Expressway #3416

McKinney, TX 75070

https://www.TeresaLusk.com

ACKNOWLEDGMENTS

I had attempted to write this book more than two years ago and only completed half of a chapter. Looking back, I am glad I waited. Life added new experiences and determinations about the heart of God for His creation. I learned that the Lord wants His people free, no exceptions. I now write from that perspective.

I want to start off by thanking many people involved in this process, but in no particular order. I want to acknowledge that I could not have completed this project without them, and I mean that with all my heart. I love you all very much!

To My daughter Sarah—Thank you for putting the final pressure to complete this project by reminding me that "I had things to do." You are one amazing young woman, and one of the best editors I have ever worked with. Love you!

To Marisella R.—The Lord brought you into this

family at just the right time, and He has blessed us with your gifting for this project and so many others. Love you!

To Angela R.—Friend, you placed a demand in me to write a book that would help in the freedom and deliverance process. Since you asked, I promised and had to complete this book. Love you!

To Jodi W.—Wow! How the Lord reconnected us through this project! I am so happy He did, because you shared your wisdom, and I was able to provide a broader perspective. You bless me! And thank you for helping with editing!

To Kristi W.—Thank you for taking the time to help me tighten up the writing! Love you, sister!

To Marguerite J., Mary R., Deborah T., Holly S.—I love you, friends, and I am beyond grateful that I was able to contact you and get your opinion on some titles!

To Vanessa X.—Thank you for being part of my writing projects in some form or fashion for years now! Love you!

To Tina W.—Thank you for your support, not just in reading my writing, but the ministry in general! Love you!

To Velia A.—Words cannot express the immense gratitude I have for the prayers you lift up to heaven for us often. This has blessed me and caused an expansion in territory! Thank you and love you!

To Dwayne A.—You were the first person the Lord used to edit my writing. Thank you very much for your effort and commitment to this project! Hugs!

To Brenda G.—Thank you for allowing the interruptions when I needed immediate editing. Love you, friend!

To Terry R.—Thank you for sharing your story that will be a blessing to many! Hugs!

To a young lady named Chloe W.—You inspired me to write a book for youth and kids in the near future. Thank you, sweet girl. Hugs!

To Pastor Dianna G.—Thank you for reading this book before its completion, even with your busy schedule. I am thankful for you and Pastor Glen and for your unconditional encouragement. Love you both!

To Shelly W.—Thank you for honest input, my friend. Love you!

INTRODUCTION AND TRAINING

The Spirit-filled life is the greatest gift the Lord has given us, besides salvation, that manifests through a relationship with God, Jesus, and the Holy Spirit. Being submerged in a Holy Spirit experience is part of the *Spirit-filled life*. It is something so supernatural that does not make sense to the world or to our senses. This may be the only part that is missing for many: to be trained by the Holy Spirit and be unexpectedly submerged in an experience we cannot explain. You may be minding your own business one day and praying to Jesus for the person sitting in front of you, when you experience your first ever deliverance (casting out demons) training session by submersion. There are many who were baptized into this ministry by an unexpected event. This has made a way for them to begin this type of work in the ministry, only to never look back. Will you answer the commandment given to you in Mark 16:15-18 that instructs us to cast out demons, lay hands on the sick, and speak in new tongues?

Our Teacher, the Holy Spirit, will teach you things you have never known. Set your heart to hear Him more clearly. Trust His voice and the discernment He gives you. You are anointed.

The Holy Spirit has trained and taught me things that no person has ever shared. He has pointed out things I would have missed and has even provided ministry for my own freedom during my personal prayer time. Although I do not consider myself an expert and am not able to cover every single possible event or training principle regarding deliverance through the Spirit-filled life, I am sharing what is necessary to stir your spirit. Paired with stories, the Word of God will be the foundation to all that is provided. All the Scriptures we will use will be out of the New American Standard version of *The Holy Bible* (NASB). Be prepared. The Holy Spirit Himself will be training you through the most amazing, excellent, and flawless academy you could ever be a part of!

IS IT MY CALL?

THIS BOOK IS WRITTEN with a two-fold purpose. First, it is written with a deep love in my heart for those who desperately want to be free from the pains and bondage caused by demonic influences over their lives. Secondly, it is authored for those who want to lead others into freedom from these bondages and are ready to put Mark 16:15-18 into practice. Throughout the book, we will introduce and educate the reader about the *cast out demons* part of Jesus' instructions. This is often referred to as deliverance or freedom ministry.

> *"And He said to them, 'Go into all the world*
> *and preach the gospel to all creation. He*
> *who has believed and has been baptized*
> *shall be saved; but he who has disbelieved*
> *shall be condemned. These signs will*
> *accompany those who have believed: in My*

name they will cast out demons, they
will speak with new tongues; they
will pick up serpents, and if they drink any
deadly poison, it will not hurt them; they
will lay hands on the sick, and they will
recover"'

— MARK 16:15-18

Although this can be a controversial topic, I write out of conviction that freedom was paid for with a high price by our beautiful Savior, Jesus Christ. Many are crying out for help, and they do not know where to turn. This is a safe place to begin their journey and become *Unapologetically Free.* I will share revelations from the Spirit of God that have been experientially released into my life and by reading and examining the Word of God. You will find stories that will allow you to grasp a greater picture of the freedom others have experienced and what that can look like for yourself and others.

Through the non-theologically-heavy teaching and easy-to-understand approach, along with stories that include training principles, you will grow in understanding.

As I was composing this book, I reached out to many who have benefited from our ministry and asked if I could share their experiences. Those I contacted asked me to share everything if it will help at least one person. While that would be great for the readers, that is not how I like to approach the particulars of this ministry.

Therefore, I have decided to take portions of their stories and change some details greatly to protect their privacy and integrity. Be assured that nothing will be removed from content that is necessary for you to see the power of God and His healing hand toward His creation. The handful of information I am sharing is to provide you with a glimpse of what you may encounter someday or have already experienced and need further understanding. Allow this time to open your eyes and heart to this reality of deliverance and freedom and invite the Lord to open up a training ground for you regarding this part of the call of the Great Commission.

Furthermore, I encourage you to enter this journey with a prayerful and humble heart. I will include prayers throughout this book to prepare you for a beautiful season of rest and liberation. For those who have administered freedom and deliverance to others, I ask that you come in with a ready stance to take in something new and fresh that the Holy Spirit would want to deposit in you. To anyone who has never heard about or explored freedom and deliverance ministry, this is a great time to invite the Lord to express a part of Himself that He desires for you, me, and others. I am excited at the possibility that through you, many of God's people will experience a level of healing for the soul, body, mind, and spirit, because God wants us all liberated. After all, *"And you will know the truth, and the truth will make you free"* (John 8:32).

3

COUNSELING, DISCIPLING, OR DELIVERANCE

I HAVE HAD the privilege of studying professional counseling and pastoral (biblical) counseling. Each of these trainings are helpful for the Christian life and can be utilized in many situations; however, they are not enough to provide complete healing, even if they all serve a purpose. Professional counseling does not have the best reputation in many Christian circles because of the secular theories they are built upon. After studying the field, I have learned it is best to take in what is good and spit out the rest. Pastoral or biblical counseling does not have as much of a negative reputation, but some Christians still believe it is not necessary to have any sort of counseling, even if it is pastoral. My biblical take on all the differing opinions and options is that we are to *disciple* people to grow into Christ's image through God's Word, and if necessary, we include deliverance ministry and pastoral counseling.

There is a shortage of Christians who are discipling others, and those who need help are not always going to attend church to get what they need, so more often than not, professional counseling is people's go-to. As a society, we are more likely to accept mental disorders as normal, but the spiritual side of the human being demands attention as well. I wonder how many devils have been labeled disorders, or how many demonic occurrences have been dismissed as hallucinations or simply part of the imagination. I am not discounting mental health, as it has its place, but I am shining the light on an opportunity of healing. I hope to bring revelation to some spiritual matters that are often overlooked by Christians but need to be identified in order to experience true wholeness for self and others.

This book may be somewhat theologically different to many who have read other deliverance books. I have respectfully addressed my take on much of what is out there regarding freedom and deliverance ministry. I would also like to encourage you to stay focused and determined in Jesus Christ if you are met with spiritual or personal resistance regarding what you are about to read. Come along with me on the journey to growing through *Unapologetically Free: Deliverance and Freedom Through the Spirit-filled Life*. Let's pray!

Prayer: Father, in the Name of Jesus Christ, the Lord of all truth, redemption, healing, deliverance, wholeness, and love, I ask You to send angels of protection over every person reading this book. Prepare their hearts to grow, learn, and be challenged, and break down barriers of doubt, traditions, and unbelief. Let Your truth guide them. Give them wisdom, open their eyes and hearts to understand, and give them determination to pass on those truths. Thank you for answering their heart's cry for more understanding of truth and freedom. In Jesus' Name, Amen.

THE DEBATE ON CHRISTIANS AND DEMONS

I WAS in the produce section at the local grocery store when my phone rang. It was a woman I knew well. "Teresa, I have to tell you a story, but you are not going to believe me." She was right. I didn't. She shared a story that angered me, as it had to do with her *deliverance,* meaning being set free from *demonic bondage,* which I didn't believe in at the time. My initial thought was that this story went along with all the drama in her life, and adding the talk about devils just kept her unhealthy cycle going.

Interestingly, a few months after the woman's phone call, I was further introduced to the concept of deliverance through a man the Lord brought into my life. In a short time, I began to introduce him to many people that needed to be set free, and I got to experience the entire process. I became a believer in deliverance and realized I had been wrong. Christians *can* be in need of freedom from demonization. It was a journey of learning I will never forget, for I had witnessed darkness being evicted and broken off many by the power and authority of the Lord Jesus Christ through His Holy Spirit.

Some have said Christians cannot be demonically *possessed*. They are right, as possession refers to full ownership of a person's body, mind, will, emotions, and spirit. *Demonization* refers to a demonic oppression outside of the body or in the flesh, but not ownership of the person's body, spirit, mind, will, emotions, or intellect. This is because they belong to Jesus and have the Holy Spirit in them.

Once I began to get a full revelation of the darkness that held so many, I repented of hardening my heart toward the broken with my unbelief. It hurts me today when I see God's people assume a pharisaic attitude, and they decide someone must not be saved, a true Christian, if they didn't overcome all bondage, weaknesses, or shortcomings at the time of salvation.Another assumption rendered from people who do not agree with deliverance and freedom ministry for Christians is that the afflicted simply need to learn obedience to the Word of God and begin to renew their mind. It is absolutely essential that a Christian not allow their selfish, godless passions to dictate their lives. Starving the desires of the flesh can set us free from the darkness at work and its oppression that was defeated at the cross and resurrection of Jesus Christ. In many cases, this is a simple matter.

With discipleship, most people will learn how to

renew their minds and begin to think, act, believe, feel, and live out their lives like Christ, in freedom. Yet, at times, there is a demonic bondage that attempts, and often successfully causes believers to keep from moving forward.

UNWELCOMING REACTIONS

These may be your initial feelings or those of others towards you because they are set in stone that they "know what they know," and that Christians shouldn't need any kind of freedom after salvation. This matter has been greatly debated for many years. We can share our views and leave the rest in the hands of God. Relationships may be shaken up, people may label you paranoid, theologically challenge you, walk away from you, or tell you that you are too focused on Satan's work. However, we are not to be ignorant of Satan's schemes (2 Corinthians 2:11). We are to appropriate the freedom for the person living in captivity!

4

SCRIPTURAL BASIS FOR DEMONIZATION

THERE ARE many Scriptures that have been utilized to support each side of the demonization argument. I have provided the most common Bible verses used to support each side, and I hope that the reader can gain further clarity and understanding.

SAVED AND SEALED

Ephesians 4:30 in the NASB states, *"Do not grieve the Holy Spirit of God, by whom you were sealed for the day of redemption."* People often ask, "If we are saved and sealed with the Holy Spirit, how can we be demonized?" First, the word "sealed" means stamped. We have a sign on us that will not be broken, indicating to the Lord, angelic beings, and demons that we will be redeemed fully when Jesus returns. We can give the devil an opportunity to accomplish his work, as Ephesians 4:27 affirms, *"...and do not give the devil an opportunity."* Some versions say, *"...do not give the devil a foothold,"* meaning a hiding place.

DARKNESS CANNOT HAVE FELLOWSHIP WITH LIGHT

The most often-quoted Scripture to deny demonization for the believer is 2 Corinthians 6:14. Well-intentioned persons will say, "Darkness cannot reside in the light," to defend their position. Let's visit what this passage actually states. *"Do not be bound together with unbelievers; for what partnership have righteousness and lawlessness, or what fellowship has light with darkness?"* This Scripture is often quoted out of context. This passage means that as believers, we have no business making *friendships* with and promoting the choices of those who give themselves over to darkness, because the two are from completely opposite sides. The darkness is the world of the unbelievers and idolaters. If you are a believer, the Holy Spirit is within you, yet you still sin. Having the Holy Spirit as a permanent resident does not mean darkness cannot play a part. We see it daily in the lives of Christians when they choose to sin on purpose.

There is an often-held belief that Satan can only keep a Christian in bondage with ties from the outside of their flesh and that casting out devils residing within a person is only applicable to nonbelievers. The other side of that argument is that a person should not have demons cast out from them, unless he or she has the Holy Spirit within them, because seven spirits more evil than the first will come in. Luke 11:24-26 in the NASB states:

> *"When the unclean spirit goes out of a man, it passes through waterless places seeking rest, and not finding any, it says, I will return to my house from which I came. And when it comes, it finds it swept and put in order. Then it goes and takes along seven other spirits more evil than itself, and they go in and live there; and the last state of that man becomes worse than the first."*

So then, would Jesus have cast out demons from those He knew would not have the Spirit to infill them? This position is hard to maintain. Freedom is for all of God's creation.

Sin Resides in Your Flesh and So Can Demons

It took one last experience with someone who was adamant that demonization could not take place in Christians for me to ask the Lord to reveal to me with no room for doubt that what I had seen and believed could be backed up biblically. I didn't want to igno-rantly disagree with people. I wanted to be able to back it up because, biblically speaking, we cannot go on experience alone. Thankfully, the Lord took me to Romans 7:14-21. This section, along with chapter 8, speaks of sin as an evil entity which resides in the flesh.

So, if sin can *dwell* in the flesh, and we also have the precious Spirit of God residing in us, why can't a demon reside in the flesh of a Christian? Read the text for yourself and see just how dark this sin that resides in the flesh of the Christian truly is.

> *"For we know that the Law is spiritual, but I*
> *am of flesh, sold into bondage to sin. For*
> *what I am doing, I do not understand; for I*
> *am not practicing what I* would *like to* do,
> *but I am doing the very thing I hate. But if*
> *I do the very thing I do not want* to do, *I*
> *agree with the Law,* confessing *that the*
> *Law is good. So now, no longer am I the one*
> *doing it, but sin which dwells in me. For I*
> *know that nothing good dwells in me, that*
> *is, in my flesh; for the willing is present in*
> *me, but the doing of the good* is not. *For the*
> *good that I want, I do not do, but I practice*
> *the very evil that I do not want. But if I*
> *am doing the very thing I do not want, I*
> *am no longer the one doing it, but sin which*
> *dwells in me. I find then the principle that*
> *evil is present in me, the one who wants to*
> *do good. For I joyfully concur with the law*
> *of God in the inner man, but I see a*
> *different law in the members of my body,*
> *waging war against the law of my mind*

and making me a prisoner of the law of sin which is in my members. Wretched man that I am! Who will set me free from the body of this death? Thanks be to God through Jesus Christ our Lord! So then, on the one hand I myself with my mind am serving the law of God, but on the other, with my flesh the law of sin."

The spirit of a saved individual belongs to the Lord, while the flesh has not yet been redeemed, which is why we will get a new and eternal body in heaven. It is my observation that many believers do not understand the biblical complexity of our flesh, soul, and the spirit. Therefore, imagining that evil could participate in our lives through our flesh, becomes overwhelming to us. Paul gave us the most visual illustration that we need to understand how a Christian could be in need of freedom and deliverance ministry.

5

GOD WANTS PEOPLE FREE TODAY

IT IS important that we understand deliverance is God's will for His people. Some call it the children's bread. Our Father sent His Son Jesus Christ so that we would experience salvation which includes emotional, physical, and spiritual healing, peace, prosperity, deliverance, freedom, and the right to be with God, Jesus, and the Holy Spirit for eternity and while here on earth.

It is *not* God's pleasure that the individuals that are hurting and bound remain that way. That would be completely opposite of the new covenant provisions the Father provided through Jesus. To be free in life and to administer freedom ministry to people, we must have a depth of understanding of the new covenant we have in Jesus, or we may leave people hurting and in bondage.

Of course, suffering exists, and we are promised the sufferings of Christ, which is *persecution and trials* for our faith. I realize that erroneous religious doctrine, rather than God's truth, has spread everywhere for years and so has the bondage that it has offered. Rightly dividing, reading, studying, and applying the Word of God is what our Father desires for you and me. This is something to be looked at with an open heart and fresh eyes to the Word of God, not with the knowledge we have acquired.

I have been met with the discussion and, oftentimes, the argument that God wants us to suffer, and that bondage is His punishment so that we can become more like Him. My questions to those who held those beliefs were very raw. "So, a woman being abandoned by her husband while she had no means of support, was so that she would become more like God?" And, "A person getting cancer is so that God could teach them how much He loves them?" I could go on and on.

The truth is clear. There is no doubt that the Lord will cause something exceedingly and abundantly good to come out of suffering, but only because He is a *good* God, not because He wanted us to suffer to teach us something. Jesus said, *"The thief comes only to steal and kill and destroy; I came that they may have life and have it abundantly"* (John 10:9-10). Nowhere in the New Testament did Jesus leave anyone He came across with their sickness, broken hearts, or their devils. He healed all *manner of disease and cast out all demons*. Do people still die while praying, fasting, believing, being prayed for, and fulfilling the Christian healing checklist? Of course. That does not make it God's will, just like all the evil that happens in the world is not His will either.

This is a moment when you and I will have to look at

the Scriptures and study them with open eyes and not by what others' teachings have said or by our circumstances. Indulge in the Word of God and see what Christ has done for us. I realize this can shake up your foundation if you have believed this way, but all things must be carefully and correctly evaluated. We must ask ourselves why we subscribe to this theology. There are many Scriptures regarding suffering that are immediately interpreted as being God's will. If we don't have the new covenant foundation straight, which demands healing and deliverance, we may leave people in bondage to devils that cause disease and sickness. This would be contrary to what Jesus did in the Gospels and what the Apostles exemplified after Jesus ascended to the Father. Assigning evil, including sickness, disease, and demonization, to Jesus would be like a house divided against itself.

> *"Then a demon-possessed man who was blind and mute was brought to Jesus, and He healed him, so that the mute man spoke and saw. All the crowds were amazed, and were saying, 'This man cannot be the Son of David, can he?' But when the Pharisees heard this, they said, 'This man casts out demons only by Beelzebub the ruler of the demons.' And knowing their thoughts Jesus said to them, 'Any kingdom divided against itself is laid waste; and any city or house divided against itself will not*

stand. If Satan casts out Satan, he is
divided against himself; how then will his
kingdom stand? If I by Beelzebub cast out
demons, by whom do your sons
cast them out? For this reason, they will be
your judges. But if I cast out demons by the
Spirit of God, then the kingdom of God has
come upon you"

— MATTHEW 12:22-28

Activating faith and firmly understanding our covenant rights and authority in Christ will allow us to become free quickly, stay free for good, and help others do the same. If we struggle to believe the truth that Jesus wants us healed and free, we may not be so quick to help the broken. If our belief system is not settled, we will be met with demonic resistance, because our faith is not lined up with the truth. You see, the enemy loves to find a kink in what we subscribe to and will gladly use it against what we are attempting to accomplish. To give you a clear glimpse of Jesus' desire for the world, we must see what He did here on earth, and identify the division between old covenant and the new covenant. The old covenant was represented by curses and sickness. The new covenant is represented by healing and deliverance. Following are some Scriptures that confirm deliverance and healing are the desire of the Lord Jesus Christ to solidify the truths of God.

SCRIPTURES

*"And He said to them, 'Go into all the world
and preach the gospel to all creation. He
who has believed and has been baptized
shall be saved; but he who has disbelieved
shall be condemned. These signs will
accompany those who have believed: in My
name they will cast out demons, they
will speak with new tongues; they
will pick up serpents, and if they drink any
deadly poison, it will not hurt them; they
will lay hands on the sick, and they will
recover'"*

— MARK 16:15-18

*"Behold, I have given you authority to tread on
serpents and scorpions, and over all the
power of the enemy, and nothing will
injure you"*

— LUKE 10:19

*"The one who practices sin is of the devil; for the
devil has sinned from the beginning. The
Son of God appeared for this purpose, to
destroy the works of the devil"*

— I JOHN 3:8

"Is anyone among you sick? Then he must call
for the elders of the church and they are to
pray over him, anointing him with oil in
the name of the Lord"

— JAMES 5:14

"They brought the boy to Him. When he saw
Him, immediately the spirit threw him into
a convulsion, and falling to the ground,
he began rolling around and foaming at the
mouth. And He asked his father, 'How long
has this been happening to him?' And he
said, 'From childhood. It has often thrown
him both into the fire and into the water to
destroy him. But if You can do anything,
take pity on us and help us!' And Jesus said
to him, "'If You can?' All things are possible
to him who believes.' Immediately the boy's
father cried out and said, 'I do believe; help
my unbelief.' When Jesus saw that a crowd
was rapidly gathering, He rebuked the
unclean spirit, saying to it, 'You deaf and
mute spirit, I command you, come out of
him and do not enter him again.' After
crying out and throwing him into terrible
convulsions, it came out; and the boy became

*so much like a corpse that most of them said,
'He is dead!' But Jesus took him by the hand
and raised him; and he got up"*

— MARK 9:20-28

*"Surely our griefs He Himself bore, and
our sorrows He carried; Yet we ourselves
esteemed Him stricken, smitten of God, and
afflicted. But He was pierced through
for our transgressions, He was crushed
for our iniquities; The chastening for our
well-being fell upon Him, and by His
scourging we are healed"*

— ISAIAH 53:4-5

6

WHY DEMONIZATION OCCURS

THE DEVIL IS A THIEF, a murderer, and destroyer, according to the Word of God. He and his workers do not require an open door, permission, or any sort of *legal right* to oppress and torment. They steal. They come in unannounced, especially if we are not filled with truth. While they are thieves, it is also true that if you play with devils, you will get new enemies, but that is not the only reason they come in to torment. They do their work *illegally*.

Since these demons work illegally, we must be certain we are not collaborating with them in their work through *our* actions. We can invite them to have influence over our lives when we participate in darkness and sin and when abuse and trauma have been present. To be more specific, one of the most common ways people become demonized is by dabbling in and practicing the occult, witchcraft, and false religions. The Bible says:

"There shall not be found among you
anyone who makes his son or his daughter
pass through the fire, one who uses
divination, one who practices witchcraft, or
one who interprets omens, or a sorcerer, or
one who casts a spell, or a medium, or a
spiritist, or one who calls up the dead"

— DEUTERONOMY 18:10-11

Some demonization can be the result of severe childhood neglect, abandonment, and abuse, and we must know it was not God's will that we suffer as children. There are parents that abandon the spiritual mandate of protection, and bondage occurs from the time of childhood. Some parents purposely subject their children to darkness, and when they become adults, they are left to deal with the aftermath. Our Father in heaven has the answer for us to be free, and He deals lovingly and gently with those who have been abused and neglected.

Emotional and spiritual abuse has its effects as well. Just ask someone who was forced to be part of a cult or someone who was pounded with condemning Bible Scriptures in the name of correction. Some of the most traumatized, tormented individuals are those who were forced to join a cult as children or to play mental and manipulation games which caused major confusion as children.

Finally, constantly satisfying lusts of the flesh (willful sin) and emotions such as hate, unforgiveness, anger, lust, and other fleshly perversions will set you up to serve the wrong master. Know the Word of God and live it as truth. It's the answer book to full freedom. If I work with someone, and they insist on staying in sin, I clearly inform them that their choice to continue in that lifestyle, whatever that might be, will once again invite the darkness they want to get rid of. A lifestyle of sin, in general, will put or keep people in bondage.

I could list every possible reason for demonization, but that would cause an over-preoccupation that is not of God. The list I provided is to give the reader a general idea of the darkness and sin I am referring to. Thankfully, the Word of God and the Holy Spirit will lead you and those who need healing to the truth, and if received as such, freedom will be the result. Having a general idea of the reasons people live in bondage is sufficient, and most know when something is off. They are simply hoping and looking for someone to believe them and help them. I pray that will be you!

7

POSSIBLE SYMPTOMS AND THE NEED FOR DELIVERANCE

PEOPLE HAVE EXPRESSED to me that they were afraid of being thought of as crazy if they said they believe they needed freedom from demonization. They wondered who would believe them. Who would understand? Is this even real? Then, there are others who know something is off but are not as aware of the demonic realm and write it off altogether.

How can you decipher if you need freedom, need to renew your mind, or both? (If you don't understand renewing the mind, I will get into that topic in detail later.) We can be certain that the children of God need to renew their minds, both young and mature believers.

> "For everyone who partakes only of milk [the
> Word of God] is not accustomed to the word
> of righteousness, for he [or she] is
> an infant. But solid food is for the mature,

*who because of practice have their
senses trained to discern good and evil"*

— HEBREWS 5:13

Those who are mature *do* what the Bible says. The infants simply *read* the Bible. We get to maturity by practicing godliness. Now that is good news, because there is hope for us all.

Not every difficult situation or circumstance is due to a dark entity. However, some general possible signs of demonization can include unexplainable sickness and disease. See the following passage: "And this woman, a daughter of Abraham as she is, whom Satan has bound for eighteen long years, should she not have been released from this bond on the Sabbath day?" (Luke 13:16). Other symptoms would be severe irrational thinking, disturbing imaginations and feelings, lingering emotional pain, physical torment, constant rejection or what seems like never-ending failure, habitual sin, nightmares, night terrors, mental and emotional affliction, and actual demonic manifestations. It may also seem like those needing liberty experience perpetual closed doors to favor, opportunity, and blessing, as well as heightened and constant fixation on issues such as depression, anger, lust, rebellion, masturbation, constant rejection from others, torment, worry, anxiety, harassment, affliction, torture, jealousy, and the list goes on.

The demoniac story is one of the most detailed passages in the New Testament regarding the need for freedom. Not every person needing freedom will need it on this level. It is important that we see the other details in this story besides the looming dark imagery. It reads:

> "They came to the other side of the sea, into the country of the Gerasenes. When He [Jesus] got out of the boat, immediately a man from the tombs with an unclean spirit met Him, and he had his dwelling among the tombs [seclusion]. And no one was able to bind him anymore, even with a chain; because he had often been bound with shackles and chains, and the chains had been torn apart by him and the shackles broken in pieces, and no one was strong enough to subdue him. Constantly, night and day, he was screaming among the tombs and in the mountains [torment] and gashing himself with stones [physical harm]. Seeing Jesus from a distance, he ran up and bowed down before Him [Jesus is the deliverer]; and shouting with a loud voice, he said, 'What business do we have with each other, Jesus, Son of the Most High God? I implore You by God, do not torment me!' For He had been saying to him, 'Come out of the man, you unclean spirit!' And He was asking him, 'What is your name?' And he said to Him, 'My name is Legion; for we are many.' And he began to implore Him

*earnestly not to send them out of the
country. Now there was a large herd of
swine feeding nearby on the mountain. The
demons implored Him, saying, 'Send us into
the swine so that we may enter them.' Jesus
gave them permission. And coming out, the
unclean spirits entered the swine; and the
herd rushed down the steep bank into the
sea, about two thousand of them; and they
were drowned in the sea. Their herdsmen
ran away and reported it in the city and in
the country. And the people came to see
what it was that had happened. They came
to Jesus and observed the man who had
been demon-possessed sitting down, clothed
and in his right mind [no more affliction],
the very man who had had the legion; and
they became frightened"*

— MARK 5:1-20

Intense? Yes. I have witnessed and partaken in freedom ministry for some who have been this intensely demonized.

Visit another story with me so we can see peaceful deliverance that was causing physical illness.

*"And He [Jesus] was teaching in one of the
synagogues on the Sabbath. And there was a
woman who for eighteen years had had a*

sickness caused by a spirit; and she was bent double and could not straighten up at all. When Jesus saw her, He called her over and said to her, 'Woman, you are freed from your sickness.' And He laid His hands on her; and immediately she was made erect again and began glorifying God"

— LUKE 13:10-13

This woman just got delivered (received freedom) from a spirit. The Bible says she did, and yet it was peaceful, and she received healing and deliverance by the laying on of hands. Freedom does not always have to be filled with intensity. We will cover more on the laying on of hands in another chapter.

WHY DELIVERANCE SEEMS DIFFERENT IN AMERICA

Deliverance may look somewhat different in America than it does in other countries. Why? Because in a large number of other countries, the residents are very aware of a supernatural world that exists in their midst. They practice and welcome it, and it is no secret or shame. They entrust their health, wealth, and relationships to witch doctors as a religious and cultural practice. They have village witch doctors and leaders, warlocks, and the full gamut.

Here in America, much of the universal Christian

church is still trying to decide if demons even exist, or if one can still speak in tongues as the Bible says we can. We are still debating women in ministry and deciding if women can step out of the kitchen and into the pulpit. The American church is still debating if God still speaks audibly, in dreams, and in our spirits. I do not say this as a belittling tactic but as a wakeup call to the American church. We are being misled by our logic. In other countries, people see manifestations as a daily occurrence. Visitations from devils and supernatural activity are the norm.

As long as we don't believe demons are real and at work, they are happy to stay out of your face most times. They will remain in your space, but they're happy to stay out of your sight. As I was watching a video with a man who has encouraged and influenced me to open my heart and mind to more of God, he challenged the audience by making mention of God expanding our spiritual comfort zone. He wasn't talking about getting over who took our seat in church. He meant to go deeper and experience God's supernatural ways. It is my yearning, my desire, and my goal to get all I can of Him here on earth. Won't you join me?

8

DELIVERANCE FOR THE FIRST TIME

Once you experience freedom ministry for the very first time, you will likely become aware that God always had complete freedom in mind for all of us. The goal is to be completely free within the first round of the deliverance experience. Still, I have witnessed people need multiple deliverance occurrences. Why, if Jesus cast out demons only one time from each person he came across, do we at times have to go through it multiple times? I believe it's because we have not been practicing faith, authority, and deliverance in our Christian lives, churches, and ministry circles like Jesus did in the Bible. Jesus knew His authority. He walked it, lived it, and shared it with His disciples. Let's take a close look.

> *"When they came to the crowd, a man came up*
> *to Jesus, falling on his knees before Him and*
> *saying, 'Lord, have mercy on my son, for he*

is a lunatic and is very ill; for he often falls into the fire and often into the water. I brought him to Your disciples, and they could not cure him.' And Jesus answered and said, 'You unbelieving and perverted generation, how long shall I be with you? How long shall I put up with you? Bring him here to Me.' And Jesus rebuked him, and the demon came out of him, and the boy was cured at once. Then the disciples came to Jesus privately and said, 'Why could we not drive it out?' And He said to them, 'Because of the littleness of your faith; for truly I say to you, if you have faith the size of a mustard seed, you will say to this mountain, "Move from here to there," and it will move; and nothing will be impossible to you"

— MATTHEW 17:14-21

Let this passage be a determination for you. We can look at this and feel like we have much to achieve, or we can meditate on it and see what we can learn from the words of Jesus. With certainty, we know that Jesus would have wanted this demon to be cast out the first time, based on how He responded to the disciples' inability to cast the devil out. We can see that the disciples had an issue with faith. Simple. We know that if we cannot get things done, faith or activation of faith may be lacking.

The good news is we can activate that faith, because Jesus said we could. So, in matters of freedom and deliverance ministry, my intention is to get people set free completely the first time we meet. Large numbers of freedom ministers highly suggest deliverance must be a process. However, we don't see a deliverance process in the Bible. Some will argue that it is the only way, because *they* have taken so long to experience their own freedom. I personally believe that our thinking and unrenewed mind has much to do with the process.

For the time being, know that God honours the process because He is faithful, but as I grow in my experience and activation of faith, I expect to see a full deliverance for that person once and for all. If a process has worked for you or someone you know, great. Let's celebrate the freedom of Christ in our lives.

Emotional healing is often tied in with a process which can take longer, and we will discuss that in a later chapter. However, prolonging an individual's sessions for months or even years as I have seen before is not healthy.

Seasons here and there of deliverance can make sense if people are being set free. Nevertheless, ongoing deliverance week after week is not. At that point, it may be about the minister, not the person. If that happens, you may want to pray and search for help elsewhere. Let's always go back to the Bible and use it as our final example and direction, as we cannot go wrong with God's sweet instructions.

SHAME AND EMBARRASSMENT AFTER DELIVERANCE

As I was putting this book together, I asked a friend, who had been through a very dramatic and intense deliverance, what she thought I should include based on her own personal experience. Her suggestion was addressing the topic of shame and embarrassment regarding deliverance as a recipient. In her prior exposure to this, she talked about how she was embarrassed that this was even an issue for her. She apologized greatly to the minister helping her because during a manifestation (when a demon shows themselves through a person), she said and did things that did not come out by her own volition. She wanted others to know that if this is their situation, they have nothing to be embarrassed or ashamed for. She wants others to be encouraged and allow the Lord to have His way and provide full freedom for the person with no regrets.

I encourage you as a recipient, minister, or both, to remember that deliverance, although taboo for some groups, is biblical, and it was God's idea before it was anyone else's. So be free to comfort those bound in shame or to receive the ministry the cross provided for them.

9

HEALING THE SOUL: THE GRACE SPACE THAT HEALS

As MINISTERS and recipients of deliverance and freedom ministry, it is imperative to understand that healing of the soul is very important. The soul contains the natural mind, will, emotions, and intellect. As Spirit-filled believers, it is easy at times to ignore the needs for healing in the soul, because we are instructed to walk by the Sprit, as the Word of God says, *"But I say, walk by the Spirit, and you will not carry out the desire of the flesh"* (Galatians 5:16). God never intended for us to bypass the needs of the soul. The Word says, *"Beloved, I pray that in all respects you may prosper and be in good health, just as your soul prospers"* (3 John 1:2). The goal is to walk by the Spirit and cause and command our soul to do the same.

The body will prosper when our soul is healthy. King David left us a few examples of commanding the soul and its role and importance. He said, *"Bless the LORD, O my soul, and all that is within me, bless His holy name"* (Psalm

41

103:1). And, Psalm 42:11 in the NASB states, *"Why are you in despair, O my soul? And why have you become disturbed within me? Hope in God, for I shall yet praise Him, The help of my countenance and my God."*

I can unashamedly admit that I have been in dire need of healing for my soul. I had a damaged, severed, and divided heart that needed mending. In fact, one of the most painful but effective healings that took place in my life was concerning my soul's condition, not a demonic spirit. When we do not live by the leading of the Spirit of God, we live by the soul's desires. If the soul is broken, the results will reflect that. Praise God this has a solution and it is found in confession.

There is something relieving and powerful that the Lord has prescribed as a healing source. *"Therefore, confess your sins to one another, and pray for one another so that you may be healed. The effective prayer of a righteous man can accomplish much"* (James 5:16). There were things I never confessed to an individual when I gave my life to Christ that were healed instantly. There were also many issues that were healed when I released them into the ears of those who knew how to offer compassion and grace. As a minister, I strive to practice listening and responding with words of healing so that those who are seeking a safe space in Jesus may find it and be restored in Him.

Most people I have personally dealt with when given an opportunity to open up, have begun to weep as if that hurt or offense just occurred, even if the offense occurred over five years ago or a month ago. Let's pray to be the ones who offer the grace space and support. In doing this, it may begin the process of what I often call mourning it out. It enables people to begin the healing and freedom process and put an end to it once and for all.

The graceful space requires a very compassionate and empathetic response to their expression of pain. The words we convey can heal or halt their progress, so when appropriate, we can say, *"I am sorry that this happened to you. It was never supposed to be that way."* Be aware that many people often get apologetic when they break down, as it can feel shameful or awkward to them.

Reassure them that you are honored that they opened up and encourage them to continue to mourn it out. As human beings, we hold back emotion so often that if we don't give ourselves permission to let go, we will visit that pain again.

Once they begin to share, I ask them a lot of questions that will provide a reality check such as, *"Is there really something you could have done about that?"* Or, "Did you know all the details of this situation before you entered into it?" And maybe something like, "What can you do today that is in your power to change this?" These may mirror counseling questions, I realize, but they provide the person an opportunity to tell themselves the truth. "And you will know the truth, and the truth will make you free" (John 8:32). It works. It's powerful. Confession, beyond issues of sin, sets others free. I use this with people and watch them heal from deep-seeded issues in only one appointment.

The second concept I implement is a simple prayer

which simply acknowledges the issue lingering in the soul. While there can be a malignant spirit attached to the pain, it is easiest to compound all the issues together and get the person an emotional release. There is not a strict guideline on how I deliver the prayer. The objective is to acknowledge the hurt embedded in the soul, identify the enemy attached, if there is one, release them from the pain and torment, and speak a state of freedom through declaration. Although I am not always aware if there is demonization issue along with the aching soul, I still address it for good measure.

An example of the prayer would be as follows:

Father, in the Name of Jesus, I thank you for healing this woman or man. You are the healer of their soul and You want them free. I thank you for restoring the broken pieces in their soul, mind, will, emotions, and heart. Let your Holy Spirit minister what only He can. In Your Name I pray.

It's very simple, no gimmicks, mostly acknowledgments. I then take the person through a prayer they say out loud. This is where I see a lot of response, and, at times, emotional or spiritual resistance regarding liberty.

The general statement I have them confess is as follows:

In the Name of Jesus, Father, I renounce all hurt regarding (blank). I renounce the hurt, anger, pain, frustration, unforgiveness, etc., and any other issue that is unknown to me but known to You, my God. I release all the issues concerning this situation and bless the (name them persons, organization, situation), and I renounce any evil or harm spoken about them or over them. I release myself from the things that do not bow their knee to Jesus. In His Name, Amen.

This can be composed as you go. It doesn't have to be scripted or rehearsed. It is a prayer practice applied by many who have practiced freedom and deliverance ministry. Don't forget to invite the Holy Spirit to guide you and address what He sees is at hand. While there can be some resistance emotionally or spiritually, it is our job to push ourselves or the person we are ministering to through to the end. I advise the recipients of ministry that if they are finding it difficult to speak, or if they feel anxiety through the situation, to call on Jesus. He is the deliverer of their soul. This approach keeps the focus on the Lord and not on an uninvited encounter with Satan's helpers. Finally, I ask the Holy Spirit to fill, heal, and restore any areas that were previously wounded.

I would like to remind the reader that we cannot as ministers and as created children of God ignore the need for healing in this area just because we are to be led by the Spirit and not the flesh. We are body, soul, and spirit. If God thought we needed all three, then all three are part of His creation, and freedom and deliverance would not be complete if we only addressed one part. When others hurt, let's be a resting and graceful place for others and lead them to refuge in Jesus. That is true ministry.

10

GENERATIONAL CURSES & THIEVING GENERATIONAL DEVILS

ONCE YOU BECOME familiar with deliverance, you may find yourself reading many books about it, watching teachings and freedom ministry videos, going to conferences, etc. In a short amount of time, you will find that every minister or person who knows how to pray for deliverance has a different theology and experiences to share. They may be similar, but rarely identical to one another. Some believe that the root of all demonic oppression is generational curses. Others hold the belief that open doors of willful sin are the cause of demonization. Some conclude it must be the Christian has some hidden, unconfessed sin. Likewise, there are those who are sure it is a combination of all the previously stated or a combination of several.

Let's look to the Bible for answers. Romans 8:2 says, "For the law of the Spirit of life in Christ Jesus has set you free from the law of sin and of death." We have been set free from the law that would be held against you and me because we are under the grace Jesus provided. The breaking of the law is what incurred the punishment and curses upon the people.

Galatians chapter three verses 8-14 states,

> *"The Scripture, foreseeing that God would justify the Gentiles [that is us] by faith, preached the gospel beforehand to Abraham, saying, 'ALL THE NATIONS WILL BE BLESSED IN YOU.' So then those who are of faith are blessed with Abraham, the believer. For as many as are of the works of the Law are under a curse; for it is written, 'CURSED IS EVERYONE WHO DOES NOT ABIDE BY ALL THINGS WRITTEN IN THE BOOK OF THE LAW, TO PERFORM THEM.' Now that no one is justified by the Law before God is evident; for, 'THE RIGHTEOUS MAN SHALL LIVE BY FAITH.' However, the Law is not of faith; on the contrary, 'HE WHO PRACTICES THEM SHALL LIVE BY THEM.' Christ redeemed us from the curse of the Law, having become a curse for us—for it is written, 'CURSED IS EVERYONE WHO HANGS ON A TREE'— in order that in Christ Jesus the blessing of Abraham might come to the Gentiles, so that*

*we would receive the promise of the Spirit
through faith."*

Go back with me to verse 10 where it states that
those who are under the law are under a curse. The curse
or curses were incurred by breaking the law, meaning
sinning against God's commandments as He revealed
them to Moses. However, the time of living under the
law with this type of penalty has passed, because Jesus
fulfilled the law.

Explore the next Scripture with me. Ezekiel 18:19-20
proclaims:

> *"Yet you say, 'Why should the son not bear the
> punishment for the father's iniquity?' When
> the son has practiced justice and righteousness
> and has observed all My statutes and done
> them, he shall surely live. The person
> who sins will die. The son will not bear the
> punishment for the father's iniquity, nor will
> the father bear the punishment for the son's
> iniquity; the righteousness of the righteous
> will be upon himself, and the wickedness of
> the wicked will be upon himself."*

This is a powerful and freeing passage. It was written
way before Jesus' crucifixion and resurrection, which
finalized the grace covenant that kept us from the curses
today. Galatians warns that we are not to put ourselves

under the law, because we are under grace. If we live under the law, then we must keep all the commandments, and breaking one is breaking them all with a penalty of a curse.

We were saved by grace by our own faith. Our ancestors' sins were not given to us to bear. We saw that very clearly in the Scripture passages. There is a lack of understanding of the Lord's grace when we are told we must find our ancestors' sins and confess them all. We get to put a stop to that when we give our lives to Christ. There is no need to go on a rabbit hunt to find unconfessed sin, because we simply cannot find every one of them. If I miss the purpose of grace, which came in place of a curse, I miss the entire good news, the gospel of Jesus Christ. *"He [GOD] made Him who knew no sin to be sin on our behalf, so that we might become the righteousness of God in Him"* (2 Corinthians 5:21).

Did Jesus pay for all your sins? The answer is yes. Did you receive the invitation Jesus provided for you to make Him Lord and find reconciliation with God through Him? I hope so. If not, you can say yes to Him right now! Say "Yes Lord, I give myself to you." So, if you are a Christian and believe, you have a right to freedom and do not have to chase after your ancestors unconfessed sin. You are free! That is good news for us and for our future generations.

My passionate pursuit to discuss this and give you an opportunity to consider the teaching is for several reasons that could change your life and that of others'. I have seen blood-bought believers live in condemnation because they can't seem to *identify* or locate the series of sins their ancestors committed. Believing this doctrine, their journey is never-ending. Every unfortunate circumstance and situation is attributed to unconfessed generational sin, never seeing the abundant blessings of God.

Secondly, living under the generational curse theology offers a very conditional view of God. It claims that if a child of God fails, they get the curse. This misunderstood doctrine has been a detriment to the believers desiring their full freedom. I have personally witnessed painful stagnation in these people's lives where deliverance ministers carry out months and years of deliverance on someone as they attempt to find all the generational curses in their family line.

I speak out of personal experience with this theology, as I once subscribed to it until I began to research the Word of God thoroughly for myself. There, I found and understood that I have a blood-bought right in Christ to be free. I could never find all the sins my ancestors committed. God is a good God, and He is not asking us to search for what we could never find. That would simply be a cruel Father, and in Him, there is no darkness at all.

GENERATIONAL DEVILS, NOT GENERATIONAL CURSES

Now that we have generational curses aside, let's discuss what I have seen at work regarding generational demonic activity. Although I do not agree with the generational *curses* theology, which says devils have a right to be in the family line because of our ancestors' sins and bringing forth the curses to us, there is illegal, generational demonic activity, that asserts its will and destruction in family lines. The difference between the two theologies is that one says, "Until we confess the past sins of our ancestors, they have a right to bring destruction." The other says, "I have been blood-bought and saved by grace. They have no right."

Remember they are thieves. Their activity in the life of the Christian is *illegal*. Our job is to evict them. They do not want to leave by choice, because they have been working in the family lines for years. The good news is we get rid of these enemies in the same manner as any other demonic entity. We command them to leave. If we encounter a struggle for them to leave, often fasting with prayer is the answer, or having someone else pray over you. I do caution you that generational devils and cycles have a way of hanging on and passing down when we *participate* in destroying our lives with them. Do not be fooled, if we are blood-bought believers but continue in the sins and cycles of our ancestors, they will remain. Not because it's a curse, but because we have given them an invitation to remain and hang out with our next generations. Let's not go back to what Jesus paid a mighty price for us to be set free from.

KNOWLEDGE OR REVERENCE

You may say, "Teresa, we were set free, and no devil

can touch me or harm me." That is the state of faith I desire for everyone to reach. I do not want any of us to be so devil-conscious that we forget that "Greater is He who is in [us] than he who is in the world" (1 John 4:4). We, however, must not be ignorant of the devil's schemes. Ignorance and fear are two different things. To fear means to revere. One day while reading my Bible, I did a word search and looked up the word fear in Psalm 23. That word happened to mean to revere. I arose with righteous anger. I never wanted to be caught revering evil. My reverence is for the Lord, and this helped me put matters into greater perspective. The Bible clearly says that Jesus came to destroy the works of the devil (1 John 3:8), and we are called to assert that victory in our lives.

Not being ignorant means we acknowledge that things happen that are not God's will. See a few examples for insight. Satan filled Ananias and Saphira's hearts to lie to the Holy Spirit (Acts 5:3). Paul attempted to visit the Thessalonian church, but he said Satan hindered him (1 Thessalonians 2:18). It has been my experience with some deliverance ministers that they practice magnifying Satan's power and ability. I don't think they mean to. I just believe they don't have a full understanding of the power of the cross and the authority of Jesus Christ, or they lose sight of the power of God in the moments of demonic resistance. It is worth mentioning again: Jesus is GREATER than anything or anyone operating here on earth.

11

DELIVERANCE MINISTRY IS FOR EVERYONE

MANY CHRISTIANS HAVE NOT BECOME acquainted with the one Scripture that commands believers to do the works Jesus did.

> *"And He [Jesus] said to them, 'Go into all the*
> *world [men, women, and young people] and*
> *preach the gospel to all creation. He who has*
> *believed and has been baptized shall be*
> *saved; but he who has disbelieved shall be*
> *condemned. These signs will accompany*
> *those who have believed: in My name they*
> *will cast out demons, they will speak with*
> *new tongues; they will pick up serpents,*
> *and if they drink any deadly poison, it will*
> *not hurt them; they will lay hands on the*
> *sick, and they will recover'"*

— MARK 16:15-18

The Spirit-filled ministry is a command to *all* who believe. Yet some want to ascribe this only to the anointed. *"But you have an anointing from the Holy One, and all of you know the truth"* (1 John 2:20). All of us who believe in Jesus have His anointing, and we have the commandment to go. The obsession with believing only certain people can fulfill Mark 16 has separated Christians in Charismatic, Spirit-filled, Pentecostal, and non-Spirit-filled circles. It has built a lie that unless someone has laid hands on you or passed on a mantle, you as a blood-bought child of God cannot practice deliverance or pray for the sick. I personally know non-Charismatic, non-Pentecostal, believers who do not believe in the active work of the Holy Spirit and His gifts according to 1 Corinthians 12:7-11, yet they cast out demons. A number of Spirit-filled believers cannot wrap their minds around this, as I could not for a long time.

God is not a respecter of persons. He wants the captives free and He loves all His creation.

I realize that some people are naturally daring and bold and run to things that would cause most of us to turn as fast as we can. However, that is not permission to deny the call. There are some to whom God has revealed many things regarding deliverance. He has allowed them to experience situations that would be unbelievable to many, yet we are all equally called and qualified.

The most exciting stories I have heard regarding deliverance, come from those who did not believe in it to begin with or believed it was only for the special few. These individuals have expressed the most radical stories ever heard.

There was one story a couple of weeks before the writing of this book. It was a husband and wife who were having marital issues and expressing that contention with their words to one another. Within moments of the situation, the wife manifested demonically. She became belligerent, offensive to him and toward herself, as is common in a manifestation. Within a moment, she became aggressive, and her eyes were rolling back.

The words that were being spewed were full of death. Thankfully the husband knew the Word of God, and he began to quote it to this demon, and commanding that it leave his wife. After nearly two hours, it left her.

The boldness of the Holy Spirit rose up within the husband. He expressed to me that he did not experience fear, but rather righteous anger. *"The wicked flee when no one is pursuing, But the righteous are bold as a lion"* (Proverbs 28:1). Although fear did not overtake him, he was astonished at the situation and revelation he now had. He said to me, "I never entirely bought into the whole demon thing."

The interesting thing is that this had happened before when he dismissed it as anger management issues. He had heard about deliverance but hadn't opened his eyes to the realities of it all. I asked him to share any words of wisdom for those who do not believe in demonization or believe that it is only for certain people. He said, "I was on that same side with the others that say it is only for a select few. Since this happened, I am convinced that as long as you believe in Christ, this is for you too!" Amen!

When he shared the events that occurred with me over the phone, I had such a joy in my heart. I was so excited that the Lord would allow a non-believer in this subject matter to get to practice deliverance ministry with little to no knowledge or belief that this was real. I congratulated him and told him he was going to be doing more of the freedom ministry as was his beautiful wife. She too has so much to offer and nothing can take this experience from her after what she has been through. I am looking forward to the many who will receive freedom through this couple and their experience.

MEN AND WOMEN ARE EQUALLY CALLED

For years, many Christian circles have promoted a partial gospel and taught, asserted, and enforced that the call to ministry is for men only. The narrative vehemently suggests that women can teach a Bible class for children, serve in the kitchen, and other small administrative tasks, but the spiritual work is for the men. When we rightly divide and study the gospels, we see that Jesus undertook the breaking of these traditions in plain sight of the religious, such as the Pharisees and Sadducees, who were very legalistic.

I am thankful that at the cross, Jesus set women and men free, and the commission of the believer was given to *everyone*. In fact, when we visit the Bible from the old covenant all the way to the new covenant, we see that women had many more rights than we may be aware of today. There were prophetesses, women who spoke by the inspiration of the Lord God all the way back in the Old Testament. There are commentaries that have minimized the word prophetess to a prophet's wife. This is not at all accurate. Women were on God's mind from the beginning, and we forget that at the cross and resurrection, Jesus set women *completely* free, just like our brothers in Christ.

Moreover, married women did not have their God-given rights to serve God in ministry taken away when they got married as some believe. The married woman, I have heard being said, needs permission or to be released by her husband to do any type of work. Other erroneous opinions include that she should not be allowed to pray over her husband, as he should be the one to pray because he is head of the home.

Unfortunately, there has been an ongoing oppressive and demonic agenda from the beginning that is expressed through this theology. Satan has used men and women to keep the twisted rhetoric going and binding the hands of women who are fully sealed with the power of the Holy Spirit. Let's allow the Bible to speak for itself and see what the Lord intended for women from the beginning.

Women, both single and married, fulfilled many different positions including those of spiritual leadership. We see a good number of prophetesses including Huldah in 2 Kings 22, Anna in Luke chapter 2, and Deborah, the judge and prophetess who ruled over Israel as stated in Judges chapters 4 and 5. Then we have Junius, a rarely mentioned, underappreciated female apostle mentioned in Romans 16. How about Hannah? A woman and mother dedicating her child to the work of the Lord in 1 Samuel 1. This meant the child was to be left under the direction of the priest and prophet, and she and her family would probably only see their child once a year during sacrifices. Yet, this woman made that commitment without her husband's approval. This was during a time when we see women in a much more oppressive state due to cultural expectations.

We also have entrepreneurial women running more than one business including the Proverbs 31 woman and Lydia the fabric distributor (Acts 16). I once heard someone say that the Proverbs 31 woman was a compilation of women because one woman could not have fulfilled all that Proverbs 31 says she did. And this is where the women giggle. We have Phoebe the Deaconess who is often incorrectly labeled as a servant but not a leader. While her work as a deaconess is often minimized to servant rather than spiritual leader and worker like the rest of the men in the new covenant, we have even greater evidence that the Lord wants and always has intended for women to partake of His work.

My question to any who resist the freedom of women for any position she is called to, including that of Apostle, Prophet, Evangelist, Teacher, and Pastor, is, "Did Jesus set everyone free or only our brothers in Christ?" The answer is *all*. If she is married, the fact that her husband is the head of the home does not nullify her qualification in any way. Priscilla and Aquilla are examples. Her name is listed before his at least once, which is untraditional. She taught the man named Apollos the better way of the Lord, as did her husband (Acts 18:26).

Several years ago, I read a book written by an evangelist from another country. He stated that in his deliverance crusades, if someone manifests a demon, a female assisting in the crusade may attempt to get things under control by calling a man over, who is also serving, to come and cast the demon out. She is only to do so much, then the man can perform his calling. What a lie that has many bound! Satan loves that women are oppressed with our fellow believers' thinking. "But for now, ask yourself: What is God's absolute principle that should guide all of our thinking concerning men and women? It is equality. Absolute equality" (Cunningham & Hamilton, 2000).

Be free, women of God! You too were called and fully qualified. Men and women, if you struggle in this area, remember God set us all free. "There is neither Jew nor Greek, there is neither slave nor free, there is neither male and female; for you are all one in Christ Jesus" (Galatians 3:28). This is the Word. It is clear, women have the same commission and they too can preach, prophesy, set the captive free, pastor, and do any other work the Lord assigns.

If we read the New Testament where Jesus deals with women, it is compassionate, empowering, and empathetic. "I am telling you disqualifying our women from leadership is costing our cities" (Vallotton, 2013). It's not only costing our cities, but it is hindering them from advancing the Kingdom of God as He instructed them to do as well. Three of the greatest books I have read that help women heal from the pain of oppression and restrictions in ministry are *Fashioned to Reign* by Kris Vallotton, *Women of Destiny* by Cindy Jacobs, and *Ten Lies the Church Tells Women: How the Bible Has Been Misused to Keep Women in Spiritual Bondage* by Lee Grady. These books hold so much truth and will equip you to minister freely and allow others to do the same.

LET THE HEAD OF HOUSE PRAY

The question regarding the husband being the only one who has authority to pray regarding demonic activity in the family or home has come up before. Along with what I addressed above, this too has been greatly misunderstood. When we give our lives to Christ, whether we are single or married, we as individuals made that decision. Our spouses cannot get saved for us. When we said or say yes to Jesus, the Lord provides us all who believe with the power and authority of Jesus Christ through the Holy Spirit. In the home, even if the husband is to stand in a protective, prayerful, stance regarding his family, it never cancels or makes inferior the wife's post.

One of the most beautiful positions we can adopt as believers is that husband and wife are *one*. "And the two shall become one flesh; so, they are no longer two, but one flesh" (Mark 10:8). The marriage relationship can be made to look like a curse rather than God's blessing. God did not intend for marriage to look one-sided. I have witnessed how many relationships operate with unbiblical, unhealthy rules, and the wife is under her husband's feet because religion said so.

Women and men are both given the Great Commission, so let's be obedient and be free to act. My husband and I have done freedom ministry together and separately. I did not have the option to sit back quietly, because God has called me, just as He called my husband. I get to be a part of setting the captives free, because Jesus told me so. There is something sweet and protective about my husband's presence, and I love how God blessed him with that. He also maintains an understanding that as my husband, he is to encourage me to answer the call of the Lord, and neither one of us stands in each other's way in the call to minister. As his wife, I do the same. He has so much to offer, and I love seeing him utilizing his gifts. As spouses, we submit one to another as the Word instructs in Galatians 5:21, right before instructions for the wife to submit to her husband and for her husband to love his wife. This often gets missed, yet it is the foundation for each married couple. Let husband and wife respect, honor, love, and exhort each other.

12

TRADITIONS, RULES, AND REGULATIONS FASTING

SOME SAY a person who has not fasted and prayed should not be casting out demons. They get that from a story in the book of Mark. Although I have already shared this Scripture, it is necessary to share it in light of teaching on the requirement to fast if we are performing deliverance.

> *"When they came back to the disciples, they saw*
> *a large crowd around them,*
> *and some scribes arguing with them.*
> *Immediately, when the entire crowd saw*
> *Him, they were amazed and began running*
> *up to greet Him. And He asked*
> *them, 'What are you discussing with*
> *them?' And one of the crowd answered*
> *Him, 'Teacher, I brought You my son,*
> *possessed with a spirit which makes him*

mute; and whenever it seizes him, it slams him to the ground and he foams at the mouth, and grinds his teeth and stiffens out. I told Your disciples to cast it out, and they could not do it.' And He answered them and said, 'O unbelieving generation, how long shall I be with you? How long shall I put up with you? Bring him to Me!' They brought the boy to Him. When he saw Him, immediately the spirit threw him into a convulsion, and falling to the ground, he began rolling around and foaming at the mouth. And He asked his father, 'How long has this been happening to him?' And he said, 'From childhood. It has often thrown him both into the fire and into the water to destroy him. But if You can do anything, take pity on us and help us!' And Jesus said to him, "'If You can?" All things are possible to him who believes.' Immediately the boy's father cried out and said, 'I do believe; help my unbelief.' When Jesus saw that a crowd was rapidly gathering, He rebuked the unclean spirit, saying to it, 'You deaf and mute spirit, I command you, come out of him and do not enter him again.' After crying out and throwing him into terrible convulsions, it came out; and the boy became so much like a corpse that most of them said, 'He is dead!' But Jesus took him by the hand

*and raised him; and he got up. When He
came into the house, His
disciples began questioning Him privately,
'Why could we not drive it out?' And He
said to them, 'This kind cannot come out by
anything but prayer'*

— MARK 9:14-29

Some versions of the Bible add the words "by prayer
and fasting." It is argued by scholars if the part on
fasting is even in the original manuscripts. Although we
will leave that to the scholars, we need to understand
something in order that the enemy will not accuse us.
Mathew 17 makes it clearer that the fasting and prayer
are more about lack of faith than anything else that has
been interpreted. Simply put, fasting is not a general
requirement to pray for people to be set free. If that is
what you feel you must do, then do it, because it is
according to your faith, and the enemy will play on that,
leaving an opportunity for distraction. To demand
others fast first, however, is not what we see in the
Scriptures.

Have I ever fasted before ministering deliverance?
Absolutely, but not often. The fasting was to close the
door on all my natural and fleshly focuses and to stir my
faith up for the healing of the people. God already gave
us all that we need to do His work, and I strive to
operate in that truth. If fasting is my habit before
administering freedom to someone, then I am putting

my faith in my fasting. In this case, if someone before me needs deliverance while my tummy is full, I may just deny them the freedom they need, because I didn't fast before praying for them. Instead, I choose to operate in the authority Jesus gave us.

I have heard of individuals not allowed to participate in the prayer or altar ministry at church unless they had been fasting. Living a godly life is understandable and necessary, but some restrictions have gotten out of hand in the Christian circles. My heart is to set people free from the rules and traditions that have kept the believers from walking in the Christ-given commandments.

SINNERS CANNOT CAST OUT DEVILS

Another common belief is that sinners cannot cast out devils. Grace empowers us to live a life free of sin. If your goal is to sin and to minister, take a pause. You don't understand grace yet. Still, many have sin hidden in their hearts. They may not be actively sinning with their body or stealing, murdering, fornicating, etc., but maybe they have unforgiveness and bitterness that the natural eye cannot see. They are sinning in their *heart*. Should they minister deliverance since we cannot see their sin? That is the expectation when we say the evident sinners must not set others free, but the secret sinners can proceed. There is some wisdom in this; however, I have seen some imperfect ministers set many free.

I recently spoke with someone about this very thing.

We discussed the open doors, in other words, willful sin in their life. I asked them if they had sin in their life the day they did deliverance on someone. Yes, they did. They had used words that were inappropriate and let anger have the best of them, but they were still able to set someone free. I am not suggesting a life of sin. If you are living a life of sin and think it is okay, you are missing the true grace of Jesus and should repent (change your mind about your behavior). Confess it to someone and decide in your heart to be free.

It is possible that a demon may speak forth and accuse the deliverance minister during a freedom session. They may accuse the one ministering of things that may or may not be true. That cannot cancel your command for them to leave, even if they resist. Deliverance is through authority and faith in Christ, because The Father qualified us to cast out demons through His Son. Remember, it is about *the people* in darkness. God, through His Holy Spirit, will directly convict us of righteousness and remind us we are not to be bound by sin. I do call you or those ministering to live a holy life worthy of the calling we have received (Ephesians 4:1).

It is saddening to see many proclaim Jesus and live like the unsaved. The lost often attempt to disqualify Christ, because we don't always represent Him well. If that is you, I encourage you to pray now and ask the Lord Jesus to give you a love for righteousness and a hate for works of unrighteousness. *"The fear of the* LORD *is to hate evil; pride and arrogance and the evil way and the per-verted mouth, I [The Lord] hate"* (Proverbs 8:13). Ask for forgiveness for any purposeful acts of sins that you have made into a lifestyle. People will trust you much more and the enemy, Satan himself, his workers, and your conscience cannot condemn you! Remember, even in your weakness, The Lord invites you to draw near.

> *"Therefore, since we have a great high priest*
> *who has passed through the heavens,*
> *Jesus the Son of God, let us hold fast*
> *our confession. For we do not have a high*
> *priest who cannot sympathize with our*
> *weaknesses, but One who has been tempted*
> *in all things as we are, yet without*
> *sin. Therefore let us draw near*
> *with confidence to the throne of grace, so*
> *that we may receive mercy and find grace to*
> *help in time of need"*
>
> — HEBREWS 4:14-16

13

BY AUTHORITY TO COMMAND WITH A WORD

"But Jesus rebuked him, saying, 'Be quiet
and come out of him!' And when the
demon had thrown him down in the
midst of the people, he came out of
him without doing him any harm"

— LUKE 4:35

I CAN TELL you from multiple experiences, and of
course, Jesus' example, this works. This is not the "save
their integrity" kind of deliverance. It is exactly what
you see that it is, a command! Some people who practice
and understand deliverance do not like this way of doing
things, because they don't want to embarrass anyone.
Others will say you don't need to yell at a devil and get
to hootin' and a-hollerin', as we would say in Texas.

Although there are many and often lengthy but effective deliverance practices out there, the clear biblical practice of casting out demons and setting people free is commanding them to leave because of the authority in Jesus Christ. Most other forms and methods of practicing deliverance have been learned and experienced through testing different methods by those who are involved with helping people receive their freedom.

I am not entirely opposed to some of the lengthier forms of deliverance out there, but my heart is to get back to the roots of the gospel and set people free from all oppression and bondage within one moment of exposure to the authority, Spirit, and power of the Lord. The Lord Himself left us with an important example to the believer as we see in this Scripture:

> *"When evening came, they brought to Him many who were demon-possessed; and He cast out the spirits with a word and healed all who were ill. This was to fulfill what was spoken through Isaiah the prophet: 'HE HIMSELF TOOK OUR INFIRMITIES AND CARRIED AWAY OUR DISEASES'"*
>
> — MATTHEW 8:16-17

Jesus set people free with a *word*. What word? I do not know, but it is certain that whatever word He used, whether "go," "enough," "out," or any other word, the reason it worked is that He had *authority*. Jesus said, *"I have given you authority to trample on snakes and scorpions and to overcome all the power of the enemy; nothing will harm you"* (Luke 10:19). The Lord gave us authority to cast out demons with a command. There are other examples of Jesus and the Apostles commanding devils to go, and you can read about these in the books of Mark, Luke, Acts, and Mathew.

Faith Versus Authority

Faith and authority are not the same things. *"Now faith is the assurance of things hoped for, the conviction of things not seen"* (Hebrews 11:1). Faith comes from a belief you have in God and His Word. If you believe Luke 10:19 and Mark 16:15-18, your faith will be activated, and you will get things done according to what you think you have a right to execute.

You will act and obey from a point of "I believe" versus "I have been legally sent," which is the basis of authority. Authority comes from a heavenly governmental directive given to us by Jesus. When we do the work of the Lord, if we lack faith, we can still operate in authority. If we lack the belief that we have authority, we can still operate in faith.

Your Presence

Jesus' presence alone commanded devils out of hiding:

> *"While the sun was setting, all those who had*

any who were sick with various diseases
brought them to Him; and laying His hands
on each one of them, He was healing them.
Demons also were coming out of many,
shouting, 'You are the Son of God!'
But rebuking them, He would not allow
them to speak, because they knew Him to be
the Christ"

— LUKE 4:40-41

Can this really happen with our presence alone? Yes, because the Holy Spirit resides in us. There is something powerful that manifests from the inside out when we become so firmly established in the charge we have in Christ and understanding the authority that comes from the Holy Spirit within us.

When Christ-followers live in the awareness of the Holy Spirit in them and the identity in Christ they possess, knowing the Father loves them and calls them His, this manifestation of demons by your presence alone may become much more common. This is not confined to occur only in church settings.

This happens outside of the church as well. For example, a woman we will call Maria understood well the commandment to all believers in Mark 16:15-18. She walked and operated in this truth, and one day while running errands, she stopped at the store for some needed items. As she walked by a random man, he manifested demonically in her sight and made it known by his eyes rolling back right in front of her.

Following is another story to help understand this concept. I was at a deliverance meeting and the man who was going to receive freedom ministry sat down in front of me and immediately blanked out with tears rolling down his eyes. We were at the *introduction* stage, nothing else. His breathing became intense, and he would not respond when I called his name. This man had a severe unforgiveness and hate for women, and he had a demon that intensified this hate. Eventually, after calling his name, he became aware of where he was and refocused.

Many deliverance ministers can attest to the fact their presence alone irritates people's demons. They see it in the spirit and in the natural. When this kind of things happens, and you are discerning, you will begin to see it more often than not. It doesn't always show up like some exorcist movie event, it can be a subtle thing that can be picked up through the eyes of the person, and at times, even a smirk, or a swelling of a person's face. This could seem a bit petty, but the longer you minister in deliverance, the more you begin to pick up on these things and recognize where they are coming from and why they are occurring.

Preaching

Preaching the Word of God can invite freedom to occur. This is one of my favorite forms of deliverance because hearing truth sets people free. *"And He [Jesus] went into their synagogues throughout all Galilee, preaching and casting out the demons"* (Mark 1:39). When I preach, I am very aware that the persons who hear my voice filled with Scripture and truths revealed by the Spirit of the Lord Jesus Christ will be free.

I have no doubt that when I speak truth, chains will break, hearts will heal, bodies will heal, minds will be renewed, salvations will occur, and anything else the Lord desires to accomplish will happen.

If we set our hearts to speak with purpose and partner with the Holy Spirit, we will be a conduit for the freedom that the person listening to the message needs. In other words, when you speak, don't just *speak*, be aware and discerning that what you say is alive and working, uprooting, and replanting.

Here is the vision I want you to begin to run with: "See, I have appointed you this day over the nations and over the kingdoms, to pluck up and to break down, to destroy and to overthrow, to build and to plant" (Jeremiah 1:10). This is liberty for the captives. You will witness deliverance happening in your very sight.

Preaching isn't just at the pulpit, it could be in a room discipling a person as well. This works anywhere, whether in a large or small setting, in a home, a church, a mall. It works.

Our Lord said, *"Truly, truly, I say to you, he who believes in Me, the works that I do, he will do also; and greater works than these he will do; because I go to the*

Father" (John 14:12). We often have a hard time believing Jesus at face value. He said it. Believe it!

CONFESSION

Jesus did not ask anyone to confess their sin before He set them free. He set them free and this was even before grace came through the cross and resurrection as we see in the gospels. Yet, the Word of God states, *"Therefore, confess your sins to one another, and pray for one another so that you may be healed. The effective prayer of a righteous man can accomplish much"* (James 5:16).

Some who diligently study the Word of God have said that this passage means confession is the access point for healing to come. I say confession of sin is *one* of the answers to liberty, but it is not always the answer for the person to become free. How do we know that? Jesus left us many examples of deliverance with no prerequisite at all.

There are times some situations require one to confess sin because they believe that is the only way to get healing and deliverance. Or, if you can't seem to get the person free or healed no matter what you do, then confession is a wise option. However, we must be careful not to oblige individuals to confess all their sins and find those lost and old sins before finding healing. This is why we must consider all the biblical options as we see below:

"But Jesus went to the Mount of Olives. Early

*in the morning He came again into the
temple, and all the people were coming to
Him; and He sat down and began to teach
them. The scribes and the Pharisees brought
a woman caught in adultery and having set
her in the center of the court, they said to
Him, 'Teacher, this woman has been caught
in adultery, in the very act. Now in the
Law Moses commanded us to stone such
women; what then do You say?' They were
saying this, testing Him, so that they might
have grounds for accusing Him. But Jesus
stooped down and with His finger wrote on
the ground. But when they persisted in
asking Him, He straightened up, and said to
them, 'He who is without sin among you, let
him be the first to throw a stone at
her.' Again, He stooped down and wrote on
the ground. When they heard it,
they began to go out one by one, beginning
with the older ones, and He was left alone,
and the woman, where she was, in the
center of the court. Straightening up, Jesus
said to her, 'Woman, where are they? Did no
one condemn you?' She said, 'No one, Lord.'
And Jesus said, 'I do not condemn you,
either. Go. From now on sin no more'"*

— JOHN 8:1-11

He set her free and forgave her before she asked. I am not promoting sin. I am simply making a statement to show that Jesus set people free before confession, and He draws us to Himself through the experience of His grace. The last and most important point on the Lord setting people free first before confession is this: *"But God demonstrates His own love toward us, in that while we were yet sinners, Christ died for us"* (Romans 5:8).

Now that I made my theological point, I want to be clear that confession does work. It works, because it disagrees with the enemy and what he has to offer. It says, "I disown, renounce, and disagree with Satan." It forces the torment of the soul to be brought to the light, so the loving light of Christ can shine on the sin, shame, pain, and guilt. I practice setting people free, then we deal with renewing the mind, which is confessing our sin and lining up our thinking to God's Word. The godly behavior follows.

PRAYING IN TONGUES

Savannah is a woman who had been constantly tormented by thoughts regarding a self-hate she could not understand. The presence of this self-hate was like something that was always with her that was developed from childhood due to major rejection and constant mockery from her classmates and those she loved. Savannah knew something was wrong but did not know what to do about the situation. She knew of demons but did not think she could be oppressed in that manner because she was a Christian. Yet, she could hear this entity constantly telling her she was unlikable, and it expressed hate towards her, which she internalized daily as her own voice.

One day while spending time in her prayer closet, Savannah decided that she had had enough. She began to pray in tongues with a determination never again to hear this voice that whispered death and hate to her every day. Powerful warring in tongues came out of her while she prayed, when she felt something being yanked from the inside of her belly, and she felt free. That is when she knew without a doubt the Lord had just set her free from demonization. Savannah never felt the same way about herself again after that day, and she experienced so much more peace. She was no longer afraid to enter into relationships, because she now believed she was likeable, and she began to love and accept herself more.

If you want to understand the beautiful gift of tongues further, I have included an entire chapter later in this book to help you understand it and hopefully desire it in your own life. For now, I must address that one of the greatest healing and warfare conduits for experiencing the presence of God is praying in tongues. Deliverance can occur for you and for others through this powerful and beautiful language of God and the angels. If you have the baptism of the Holy Spirit and feel that you need healing and deliverance, begin to press into the Spirit through your prayer language and see the amazing supernatural God events that can take place.

GOD IS LORD PROCLAMATION.

Shortly after I began to write this book, I took a survey on a social media platform asking which of my friends had a passion for spiritual warfare and the topic in general. I eventually mentioned that I was writing this book on that same thread. My longtime friend Jill asked if she could read the manuscript, which I was happy to share. This led us to our conversation regarding her teenage daughter, Lauren. This young lady had been enduring spiritual warfare for quite some time. Since she is young and learning to walk out her Christian life as a daughter of the King, the enemy kept bullying her. Precious Lauren had been suffering through an over-whelming focus on the work of the enemy against her and intimidations, not knowing he thrived on that. While at times we will have to face the enemy head-on with a situation. I encouraged my friend Jill to teach Lauren how to submit full focus on the Lordship of God, which is a powerful biblical warfare stance.

Jesus, who was being *pestered* by Satan, responded with authority as we see here in Mathew 4:10, "Then Jesus said to him, 'Go, Satan! For it is written, "YOU SHALL WORSHIP THE LORD YOUR GOD, AND SERVE HIM ONLY."

We can face the enemy with words filled with the truths of God. We also have the option to submit to God first and let the rest fall off. We know we have God's permission to do both, because we see it taught in the Word. It says, *"So submit yourselves to God. Resist the* devil, and he will flee from you" (James 4:7). This is a supreme practice because what can be greater than the Lord Himself?

I shared the following proclamation so that she can submit to God and not have to directly engage with the enemy by commanding him to leave:

"Father, I proclaim that You are Lord of heaven and earth. You are mighty. There is none like You. You are the powerful deliverer. You hide me under the shadow of Your wings. I have full acceptance in Your sight. You never leave me. Your angels are assigned to protect me, because I am Your child! Thank You for the peace that is beyond what I can comprehend at this moment. God, You alone are good. Jesus, You alone are mighty. Holy Spirit you fill me with truth, comfort, and peace. Father, let Your truth prevail in Jesus Name."

There is nothing fancy about this proclamation except that is declares truths and snatches the power from the lies that are being unknowingly bought into by the person. I like to remind heaven and earth that God alone is Head of all. This leaves no room for the enemy to exalt his work in my life.

WORSHIP

It was a Sunday morning when a woman named Donna got to church. As soon as she arrived, she knew something was going on within her that she could not fully explain. For two days or more, she had been feeling a wave of deep anger toward an individual in her life. The worship began, when suddenly she felt a need to move to a secluded area as she felt something about to occur but still could figure out what that was. The worship team was playing and flowing powerfully when she suddenly felt the manifested power of the Holy Spirit fall over her as is common in Charismatic services.

She knew He was ministering to her in a way so powerful, because a feeling of fire and freedom flowed into her belly area. The song that was playing during this experience was written with lyrics regarding the Lordship of Jesus Christ, His blood, His worth, and much that exalted Jesus Christ and Him alone.

The anger that Donna was being tormented with was completely evicted, and she experienced ongoing healing and closeness to the Lord for several days after. This type of deliverance is more common than we realize. Worship is a powerful warfare tool, as we see in 1 Samuel 16 when David played the harp for King Saul while he was being tormented with a spirit. If we can find it in the Bible, it can work for us as well.

DREAMS

I love dreams. God speaks in dreams all the time, but many dismiss them as too much pizza before bedtime and assign no meaning, or they assume dreams were only for old covenant times. Can I challenge you to start evaluating and writing down what you dream? I have several journals with detailed dreams that have come to pass, warnings, events that are to come, and so much more. Dreams can also tell you if you need deliverance, if you are receiving deliverance, or if someone else needs deliverance.

There have been several individuals I have personally known who have dreamed that they are having a bowel movement. These people happened to be going through a time of freedom ministry through the Lord Himself. Other deliverance dreams have included people being bathed in a bathtub and others like this that I cannot discount.

Be aware that I am not saying every dream of a bath, shower, or the like is a need for deliverance. There have been other dreams that have been reported to me regarding dreams and deliverance, and it usually consists of something being washed, cleaned, or something unclean or gross coming out of the person.

God is good, and He will carry His freedom through completely and in any way He sees fit. For a simple, useful book on dreams, my friends Holly and Alan Smith have written *Dreams: Unveiling the Language of Heaven*. If you choose other dream interpretation books, be sure they are written in a pure and biblical foundation, as there are many secular books to choose from.

RENOUNCING DARKNESS AND UNRIGHTEOUSNESS

Renouncing means we formally declare abandonment of something we have been practicing. We renounce darkness, sin, and things we do and hide or are ashamed of. Furthermore, renouncing is not just for what is hidden, but for things we do in plain sight because of a rebellious heart.

It has been my personal experience that when I take someone through a renunciation prayer, Satan hates it and makes it known. There is something about saying, "I renounce all works of unrighteousness," that quickly disarms his work over the believer who is bound. It is such a powerful statement that I have seen people get stuck while trying to say this out loud. The individuals often but not always manifest resistance in their body. They may feel a tightening in their throat, their mouth, or in their chest.

When that happens, I command them to say it in Jesus' Name! I am not talking to the person, but to the power behind the resistance. The struggle for the person usually stops and the deliverance continues. There have been times when instead of focusing on the works of unrighteousness, I flip it and say, "I will use my body, mind, will, spirit, and emotions for works of right-eousness," and the result is the same. Either way, it works, and even if bodily manifestations are there, freedom must come!

BREAKING SPOKEN CURSES

A curse can be understood as evil summoned upon someone or darkness invoked. The Bible says, *"But no one can tame the tongue; it is a restless evil and full of deadly poison. With it we bless our Lord and Father, and with it we curse men [people], who have been made in the likeness of God; from the same mouth come both blessing and cursing. My brethren, these things ought not to be this way"* (James 3:8-10).

These curses are unleashed through the mouth and ignited with evil intent that comes out of the heart. At times, even though our intention is not to *curse*, we manage to do it because of a critical, accusatory, or gossipy character. This is a great reminder to speak blessing and not cursing to and about one another. Even in anger, we are to forbid word curses to those created in the image of God.

There is a price to pay for cursing. Whether you invoke evil to others or unto yourself by the lifeless words you agree with, the price is clear. *"Death and life are in the power of the tongue, and those who love it will eat its fruit"* (Proverbs 18:21). I don't want the result of my words to be my portion.

In deliverance, breaking word curses over people has been a very effective tool. In fact, this has triggered manifestations without me expecting them. I have been left in amazement how breaking a word curse over someone can cause demonic activity to present itself right in your sight.

BREAKING SOUL TIES

Soul tie breaking is a confession of entering into a relationship that should never have been or one that ended up in an unhealthy status that now hurts or affects the person. The goal is to break the unhealthy *tie* we have with someone emotionally, spiritually, physically, and psychologically. There is not some magic process to it. Deliverance ministers, including myself, have tried various methods and prayers, and it works. In fact, I will be sharing a story later about the effects it had on someone during a ministry session.

Soul ties are exemplified in the Word of God through a healthy, brotherly relationship between King David and Jonathan, King Saul's son, as we read in the following Scripture:

> *"Now it came about when he had finished*
> *speaking to Saul, that the soul of Jonathan*
> *was knit [bound, tied] to the soul of David,*
> *and Jonathan loved him as himself"*

> — I SAMUEL 18:1

Soul ties are mostly thought of as forming when you have sex with someone. A soul tie, however, can be formed without sexual activity. I can usually identify the moment I create these bonds with someone, as I feel it when it happens. Although not always created on purpose or knowingly, individuals often create soul ties with people who have abused them or with those who have not been the healthiest relationship for them.

I have witnessed intense occurrences during the ministry time when we dealt with soul ties, along with positive and dynamic changes.

In the simple yet powerful prayers that I have led others in, I have even witnessed spouses become closer or able to be more intimate emotionally and in other ways.

Declaration: In Jesus' Name, I break the soul tie between (name the persons). I release myself from all that has come upon, in, and around me because of my connection with them. I renounce all the effects and the work this tie has produced in me. It has to break now.

CLEANING OUT ITEMS

One way you can be certain that you are not unintentionally inviting demonic activity into your home is to ask the Holy Spirit to show you any items that do not belong. You would be amazed at the items people intentionally and unintentionally bring into their home. Most people might even have items that if you pointed them out to them, they would disregard it as unimportant or incapable of disrupting their life. This even includes jewelry, home décor, kids' toys, cartoon characters, books, and clothing.

I understand the initial response to feeling protective of your stuff, but until you have gone into someone's home who is being tormented and you personally find the "harmless" items, you will quickly realize that some things are not worth taking the risk for. This is one of those situations where I have seen people through both extremes. Some dismiss it quickly, and some become so paranoid about the items given to them, that they cannot even receive a gift that is truly given in love. Frankly, there are some items that even if given to me in love, I will lovingly dispose of if necessary. If you are wondering if you have any of items that are questionable just read the following passage:

> *"There shall not be found among you anyone who makes his son or his daughter pass through the fire, one who uses divination, one who practices witchcraft, or one who interprets omens, or a sorcerer, or one who casts a spell, or a medium, or a spiritist, or one who calls up the dead"*
>
> — DEUTERONOMY 18:10-11

The Lord gave us a guideline for the works we are not to take part in or invite into our lives, and any items that represent these practices are included. This may surprise some of you, but these practices and symbols that represent them are saturated in our culture. However, if you choose to follow the Lord wholeheartedly, even horoscopes are unacceptable, yet we minimize them as fun. God wants us all free from these practices, and He fully desires that we are alert and wise. Pray to begin to discern what is really behind items. You will never see anything the same again.

Corporate Deliverance

Corporate deliverance means that deliverance happens in a large group. This often happens in a church service or ministry event but can occur anywhere you have a group of people. I have heard mixed emotions about group and corporate deliverance. Some ministers do not believe we should execute corporate deliverance, because you won't get people fully free. It is my experience that God is bigger than we understand. We do what He tells us to do, and the rest is up to Him.

I first experienced corporate deliverance through a well-known deliverance minister and now ministry friend. This gentleman was hosting a gathering in a church around town, so I went to observe him since my heart had been stirring to learn how to host a corporate deliverance. He sang for us in his old school southern gospel style, taught based on the Word, and then began to bind and command devils to leave. I know for certain freedom was happening. This opened my heart and mind to trust that much can be accomplished in a group. Ever since that encounter, my goal has always been to get people freedom at every one of my events.

14

BODILY EXPERIENCES DURING DELIVERANCE

I KNOW of a church that hands their attendees paper bags on their way in because they expect that God is going to set their people free, and sometimes that means people will throw up. Because of their practices, I am sure they get many visitors from around the world who want to experience freedom.

Like it or not, vomiting is common evidence of receiving freedom, amongst many others. Although this is not mentioned in the Bible specifically, we know that bodily experiences happen, as there was a boy with a demon who foamed at the mouth (Mark 9:20). This shows us that many things that are not mentioned actually can happen. Some ministers, including myself, will actually forbid that kind of reaction before it even happens. We don't have to see a person vomit for them to be free, but allowing it does not make it less valid or wrong.

Another manifestation while deliverance is occurring is burping. I once ministered to someone who went through some freedom, and an hour or so after the session, they experienced a burp which they described as the loudest burp they've ever heard. I have heard this from others as well.

In addition, one could experience a tightening in the throat or chest, a pain in the head, something on the legs or feet, discomfort in the belly, and depending on what kind of spirit it is, even something in the private areas. The feelings and manifestations are numerous, and you may see and hear of some not mentioned here. More dramatic manifestations may be contortions and seen as animal-like characteristics, items moving and falling, and levitation. These are the more drastic and most common in other countries, although it happens in our areas as well.

I cannot possibly lay out every detail of each possible scenario. First, because I have not experienced every single type of situation there could be, and I don't think anyone has. However, I can tell you to simply expect the unexpected and prepare to see what you never imagined. I do not say this to glorify evil. It's intended for you to know that in the *supernatural*, which is completely natural to God and the spirit world, anything is possible. This is why faith is such a big deal, because it is the key to supernatural things, for seeing the invisible become visible and much more.

15

TONGUES, THEIR PURPOSES, AND DELIVERANCE

Praying in tongues is listed in Mark 16:15-18 as a sign for "those who believe" along with other commandments for the believer. Nothing has changed since Jesus left the instructions. These were given just before Jesus' ascension to heaven. Therefore, we know that what He instructed in Mark cannot be changed. Casting out devils is for today as is speaking and praying in tongues. I have practiced this gift as a lifestyle and seen its benefits for myself and many others.

The topic of tongues is a subject that has divided God's people into different denominations and beliefs. There have been numerous books written against tongues and its present-day existence. I do not attempt to convince anyone to believe in tongues, but it would be a disservice to those who do not have a full understanding if I brushed through this information. Allow me to share what I have found to be helpful and life-changing to many.

First, tongues are the language of God and the angels. *"If I speak with the tongues of men and of angels, but do not have love, I have become a noisy gong or a clanging cymbal"* (1 Corinthians 13:1). This is a God-created language. Tongues were God's idea, and they serve several purposes. The first purpose is often called tongues of men or tongues of fire. These tongues were and still are used to communicate God's message to others when we do not speak the same language. The Bible says:

> *"When the day of Pentecost had come, they were all together in one place. And suddenly there came from heaven a noise like a violent rushing wind, and it filled the whole house where they were sitting. And there appeared to them tongues as of fire distributing themselves, and they rested on each one of them. And they were all filled with the Holy Spirit and began to speak with other tongues, as the Spirit was giving them utterance. Now there were Jews living in Jerusalem, devout men [people] from every nation under heaven. And when this sound occurred, the crowd came together and were bewildered because each one of them was hearing them speak in his own language. They were amazed and astonished, saying, 'Why, are not all these*

who are speaking Galileans? And how is it
that we each hear them in our
own language to which we were
born? Parthians and Medes and Elamites,
and residents of Mesopotamia, Judea and
Cappadocia, Pontus and Asia, Phrygia and
Pamphylia, Egypt and the districts of Libya
around Cyrene, and visitors from Rome,
both Jews and proselytes, Cretans and
Arabs—we hear them in our own tongues
speaking of the mighty deeds of God.'
And they all continued in amazement and
great perplexity, saying to one another,
'What does this mean?' But others were
mocking and saying, 'They are full of sweet
wine'"

— ACTS 2:1-13

When we are active in ministry, working and trav-
eling to other countries and even dealing with people in
our own nation who speak other languages, tongues of
fire or of men (tongues of many languages) are very
useful. It is not limited to the situations I listed, but it is
very common in these areas. Following is a story that
will help captivate the heart of tongues of men.

Over a year ago, at the time of the writing of this
book, I attended a friend's conference. She is a powerful
evangelist and a mentor to many. At the very end of her
event she scheduled what we Spirit-filled, Charismatic

believers would call activation or altar ministry, or ministry time. This means there will be speaking in tongues, laying on of the hands, being slain in the Spirit (falling over or some other physical and spiritual response due to the Spirit and glory of God over you), and many other experiences similar to these events.

I got in line to receive ministry, and because it is common to fall backward when the power of God falls on someone, a woman named Terry stood behind me, in case I needed help. When she first got behind me, I did not know who it was. I just knew someone was there. When they were done praying for me, I turned around, and the Lord said to me, "I want you to pray together." I told her what the Lord said, and she began to pray in tongues for and with me. At first, when she started to pray, I could hear her but could not understand her until a few moments later.

All of the sudden, the woman began praying in a language that had a Spanish base. It could have been Portuguese or something that sounded close to Spanish but was not. I recognized it, because I am fluent in Spanish. When she was done praying with me, I asked her if she knew Spanish. "No," she said, "Why?" I said to her, "You were speaking a language similar to Spanish and I could understand what you were saying." I told her she was saying, "God is love and there is no fear in love." It was such a beautiful thing to hear, God was ministering to me through the tongues of men. This same woman, Terry, has a powerful story to tell that correlated with her ministering to me that day.

Terry's Story

"It was the early 90's, and it was possibly my 5th mission trip. I worked at a law office at the time, and each year I would use my vacation time and go on a mission trip that would venture to three different countries within a specific amount of time. It is called a mission trio. Normally at the end of December through the beginning of January, I would have already been on three other mission trips to Venezuela, Mexico City, and Acapulco. Argentina was the last place I was going for this trip. I honestly thought this would be my last mission trio, as it was the hardest to raise money for, and it was furthest away. Additionally, I thought I knew what to expect each time.

Amazingly, it was the most dynamic trip, supernaturally seeing what God could and would do for His people. For some reason, this trip turned out totally different before I even left the United States. I found out a week before we were to leave, due to circumstances beyond our leaders' control, we had to change the originally planned location, and the church we would be working with. Normally, we had our plan firm six months in advance and had a connection with the nationals who live there, who would go on the streets with us to interpret the language of the people. This time was totally different.

We typically would take a group of 50 English speaking people, and the church we partner with would have at least have 25 to 30 nationals who live in that country and speak the native language. We found out when we got to Argentina that we would only have about 10 nationals to 50 English Speaking individuals. In the past, and for this mission trip, we all learned a short introduction in Spanish to say while on the streets and while going door to door that would open an opportunity to witness. We played a recorder with the salvation message in Spanish, then prayed with them without delay, that they may give their life to Jesus Christ.

It was amazing when we went out on the streets and saw God show up for the people. We were in groups of twos while we played the salvation message, then pointed to the question on a paper, asking if they wanted to give their lives to Christ. We would witness and feel the presence of the Holy Spirit, and with tears rolling down the people's cheeks, they would receive Christ.

On this particular trip to Argentina, we got to work with missionary Steve Hill. This was before he came to the states and preached a seven-year revival in Pensacola, Florida. Steve moved in the miraculous even years before I met him. He would talk to people, and then I would start speaking and praying in tongues after him. This went on for at least five minutes where it felt like I was carrying on a conversation with a particular gentleman we had been talking with.

There happened to be another man accompanying this particular gentleman, whom we originally began talking with, and the accompanying friend began to raise his own hands and kept shouting, "Alleluia! "Alleluia!" over and over while my partner who was saying with excitement, "You are speaking Spanish, you are speaking Spanish!"

It was later confirmed by several other episodes of this experience that I was preaching the gospel in clear Spanish. This was only *one* of the amazing experiences regarding this purpose of tongues. To God be the glory! God is good, and His gifts are irrevocable."

After praying with me, Terry shared that story with me. You see, she had been praying that God would confirm and allow her to see if He would move in that same way again and pray in tongues of fire (tongues of men) after her experience in Argentina. The answer was, "Yes." The Lord works for the good of those who love Him and need Him. The Lord will be faithful, and will continue to move through Terry, you, and me!

INTERPRETATION OF TONGUES

If you are new to the concept of tongues, you might be wondering how I knew what she was saying. I interpreted by the same way the people in the second chapter of Acts were able to understand, by the Spirit and will of God. Interpretation of tongues is considered a gift, or a grace of the Holy Spirit, a spiritual act as listed in 1 Corinthians chapter 12. This is something anyone can do by the will of God, and by the power of the Holy Spirit. It is not something to try to make logic of and solve the puzzle. I wasn't focusing on interpreting. I was listening and receiving what the Lord was releasing into my own life. Let's keep building your faith regarding tongues through another story.

We were in our Sunday morning church service. The worship was powerful, and the Lord was taking care of business and delivering individuals in a big way during this season. Now, I realize we don't all have great singing voices, but you can definitely tell when someone's key is way off. This day, there was practically a screeching coming out of a woman, we will call Darla. We escorted Darla to another room, per the pastor's instruction.

We explained to her that she was demonized, and she was quite unaware of it all. The pastor who was doing much of the freedom ministry began praying in tongues for her. I was interpreting the tongues, and the pastor was commanding Satan, in tongues, to let this woman go. The tongues were much like Spanish, even though that pastor did not know a thing about the language.

SPEAKING MYSTERIES

Another purpose of tongues is speaking to God in mysteries. The Bible says, *"For anyone who speaks in a tongue does not speak to people but to God. Indeed, no one understands them; they utter mysteries by the Spirit"* (1 Corinthians 14:2). If you research the word mysteries, it means hidden things. There are times when I feel a heavy burden about something. I have learned that that is the Lord's prompting for me to pray in tongues about someone or something, that is unknown to me.

There have been many times when I have had to pray for days because whatever was going on required my prayer until the darkness or difficult situation operating had ceased or been resolved. I learned how to work this by trust and practice. The Holy Spirit tells us when to pray and when we should stop.

Praying mysteries is not limited to the example I just gave. I believe there are many more things that come along with this. If what we are praying about are hidden things, then I can only imagine the revelation that comes after praying in tongues regarding mysteries.

Tongues that Edify the Church

Although speaking in tongues with interpretation to edify the church is the last teaching I am going to thoroughly develop, I will briefly share other things worth mentioning.

> *"One who speaks in a tongue edifies himself; but one who prophesies [speaks divine inspiration] edifies the church. Now I wish that you all spoke in tongues, but even more that you would prophesy; and greater is one who prophesies than one who speaks in tongues, unless he interprets, so that the church may receive edifying"*
>
> — 1 CORINTHIANS 14:4-5

Paul made it clear, the purpose of speaking in tongues at church is to edify (build up) the church, which is why the interpretation is required. Some churches will not allow speaking in tongues at all unless there is someone interpreting, or if that same person has the tongue and interpretation. If we are going to address the entire church in a tongue, we need the interpretation, which the Spirit of God gives through the person speaking the tongue or someone else in the congregation. God didn't intend to do away with tongues, He wants His people to understand what tongues are for, and what they are accomplishing. Otherwise, we miss the point and the power.

There is nothing unbiblical about praying in tongues while we worship at church, or in corporate prayer time. Paul told the church, *"Therefore, my brethren, desire earnestly to prophesy, and do not forbid to speak in tongues"* (1 Corinthians 14:39). Somehow that is exactly what has happened.

Not only has it been forbidden, but it has also been dismissed as something that has ceased, and attacks have been unleashed against those who still practice these giftings. God's word does not say that tongues ceased.

> *"Love never fails; but if there are gifts*
> *of prophecy, they will be done away; if there*
> *are tongues, they will cease; if there*
> *is knowledge, it will be done away. For*
> *we know in part and we prophesy in*

*part; but when the perfect comes, the partial
will be done away"*

— 1 CORINTHIANS 13:8-9

The perfect is the end of all things, completed based on the Lord's return in its entirety for all humanity. Paul stated that it was to come, *not* that it had already come. Until we become and fulfill what God intended for us, tongues, knowledge, and prophesying are necessary, even if they are only in part.

Now that we understand that tongues have not been done away, we can address the interpretation of tongues to edify the church.

*"Therefore let one who speaks in a tongue pray
that he may interpret. For if I pray in a
tongue, my spirit prays, but my mind is
unfruitful. What is the outcome then? I will
pray with the spirit and I will pray with
the mind also; I will sing with the spirit
and I will sing with the mind also"*

— 1 CORINTHIANS 14:13-14

Notice he said in verse 13, "Pray that we may interpret." How will we interpret? He prayed in the Spirit, then in his mind, which would be his native language. This is how I have seen interpretation work at times. You will feel the interpretation rise up in your spirit.

Often it will occur after you have been praying or speaking in tongues, followed by prayer in your native language. This does not happen for me every single time but most often. I encourage you to begin to explore this further if you have never experienced it before.

OTHER POWERFUL EXPRESSIONS OF THE HOLY SPIRIT

Further powerful expressions of the Holy Spirit through tongues that myself and others have experienced are listed below, and they are certainly not limited to my list. You may already be familiar with some listed.

1. Singing in the Spirit - *"What is the outcome then? I will pray with the spirit and I will pray with the mind also; I will sing with the spirit and I will sing with the mind also"* (1 Corinthians 14:15). All that is needed is to pray in a tune and it becomes singing in the Spirit. Let Him lead the tune. It is a beautiful thing!
2. Freedom from demonic oppression can happen when we press into the Spirit through tongues.
3. There can be a weeping that occurs when praying in tongues. Some understand this as a weeping of the Holy Spirit. It feels like a burden that will not cease until you press in and travail. Then, the release comes out.
4. We can war in tongues against things

happening around us that are not visible to the natural circumstances.

5. God tells us things through tongues.

6. Tongues command demonic activity to cease and changes situations.

7. We can intercede in tongues for others, including the lost, broken, and hopeless.

8. We can have a tangible experience with the Holy Spirit while praying in tongues and become physically heavy or incapable of moving, with the manifest presence and glory of God. We can become paralyzed for a moment, fall to the floor, feel shaking, electricity, fall forward, and so many other unexplainable experiences.

9. Read the Old Testament. God moved in mind-blowing ways. He has not changed! He wants His children to experience all of Him here on earth.

10. You can pray in the Spirit to write sermons, get words of wisdom, words of knowledge, prophecy, and other things the Lord wants you to know.

11. Praying often, loud, and for a long length of time will push you to another level of tongues not visited before. You will hear many different sounds, utterances, and groanings, and even receive the interpretations. You will likely begin to experience greater sensitivity to the Spirit of

God as you practice tongues the way I just mentioned.

12. Praying in tongues will stir you up in your faith and encouragement! This is why I pray in tongues anywhere at any time!

13. You will preach and or share your faith with boldness. *"And when they had prayed, the place where they had gathered together was shaken, and they were all filled with the Holy Spirit and began to speak the word of God with boldness"* (Acts 4:31).

My husband and I attribute tongues to our continuous, faithful walk with Jesus Christ. We received the baptism of the Holy Spirit just months after our conversion to Christianity. In conversations and looking back, we have asked ourselves what has equipped us personally to walk strongly and operate in so much that the Lord has allowed us to experience. We say it is tongues and good discipleship.

16

RECEIVING THE BAPTISMS OF THE HOLY SPIRIT WITH EVIDENCE OF SPEAKING IN TONGUES

LISTENING TO PREACHING

So HOW DO we receive tongues? By hearing the preaching of the Word of God, by desiring it, or by the laying on of the hands. We know for certain that studying, reading, and becoming hungry for more of God will naturally stir and activate our faith. God's Word says,

> *"While Peter was still speaking these words, the Holy Spirit fell upon all those who were listening to the message. All the circumcised believers who came with Peter were amazed because the gift of the Holy Spirit had been poured out on the Gentiles also. For they were hearing them speaking with tongues and exalting God"*

There were speaking and listening going on while Peter was preaching a full gospel (healing, deliverance, salvation, power) that included tongues. This Scripture is where the Charismatic, Pentecostal, Spirit-filled believers get the term "baptized with the Holy Spirit" or "filled with the Spirit." When asked if you been baptized or filled with the Spirit, they are asking if you have a prayer language (tongues), or if you speak and pray in tongues.

LAYING ON OF THE HANDS

Another way to receive the baptism of the Holy Spirit with evidence of speaking in tongues is by the laying on of the hands. *"Then they began laying their hands on them, and they were receiving the Holy Spirit"* (Acts 8:17).

> *"So, Ananias departed and entered the house,*
> *and after laying his hands on him said,*
> *'Brother Saul, the Lord Jesus, who appeared*
> *to you on the road by which you were*
> *coming, has sent me so that you may regain*
> *your sight and be filled with the Holy*
> *Spirit'"*

— ACTS 9:17

TONGUES ARE A GIFT FOR ALL BELIEVERS

Are tongues only for a chosen few? Why would it be? God does not pick and choose, although many have been taught otherwise. If something does not happen right away, it does not mean no. When I know God has promised something to me and I desire it, I will watch preaching and teaching videos, read Scriptures concerning that which I have hope for, and wait, because I believe God's Word. I do caution you, any books you read or things you hear that say it is only for a chosen special few may not be the message you want to submit your spirit and ears to receive.

I have had the privilege to help individuals receive the baptism of the Holy Spirit and have witnessed God baptize in the Holy Spirit even those who didn't ask for it.

Do you already have the baptism of the Holy Spirit, with evidence of speaking in tongues? Great! I pray there was something you learned today that was not already familiar to you. I pray you will stop and pray for those who will read this book, that they may desire and receive all the Lord has for them. At this moment I am pausing the writing of this book to pray in tongues for every soul that wants this baptism.

Declaration: Father, You desire that we experience all of You, and that is exactly what I want for my life. I declare and agree that I believe in all that Your Word says it has for me. I receive the baptism of fire with evidence of speaking in tongues. I release myself from all unbelief and resistances that have been upon and around me that have resisted Your supernatural power. I free myself from all traditions of people, and religious expectations and beliefs that were never Your idea, my King and my God. I extend my hands to You now to receive your gift of the Holy Spirit fire and power in Jesus' Name!

Now begin to bless Jesus with your mouth and allow the Holy Spirit to flow through you with His words. Take your time. After all, this is a new experience. Don't doubt that words or small syllables will begin to flow. Pray often and consistently and you will see this blessing flourish. Don't get discouraged if it takes longer than you would like. The Lord will give you the desires of your heart!

17

ACTIVATING DISCERNMENT AND OTHER SPIRITUAL AWARENESS

D ISCERNMENT   EXAMINES   the   person   and   the
atmosphere in the spirit and tells you what someone
may be bound by for the purpose of healing, deliverance,
and prayer. Discernment will reveal to you if what is at
work is of God or not and even the name of that which
is operating, whether a spirit or not. Other information
discernment will point to are the different spirits at
work in an organization, a church, a city, a country,
county, or even someone's home. There is no limit to
discernment. It is information from the Holy Spirit to
our spirit and natural mind that provide us direction on
the actions to take.

Discernment is a powerful tool in deliverance, and
the great news is that because of the fullness of the Holy
Spirit within the believer, we have the grace to learn how
to discern. In the early years of my Christian walk, I was
taught to pray for discernment, and I watched it develop

strongly in my life. I encourage you to pray to develop and activate this gift to do the same. It will change how you do ministry.

Some of you may have been discerning since you were children and could feel things even back then. I was certainly that way but have now learned how to use this gift and how to pray to develop it further.

Besides prayer, the best way to activate this gift is the same way we do anything else that is important regarding who *we are* in Christ and what *we have* in Jesus Christ. Whether authority, power, discernment, etc., we hear the information to learn about it, then we can believe it, and finally, we can activate it, and it becomes evident in our lives. Be aware and ready to listen. The Lord speaks, He reveals and does not hide the information that they need to know from His children. This applies to all the kingdom principles that God wants us to get hold of.

At times, I still pray for discernment as I could always develop it more, and if someone I am working with is all over the place spiritually and emotionally, it helps me stay focused.

One thing to be cautious about regarding discernment is that even if one becomes really good at discerning, the truth is we can still miss it. This can push us into a critical and accusatory spirit.

I have met several individuals who use their discernment to decide what they believe about people or to accuse them of things that are not always accurate, especially when they are offended. Let's train our spirit to discern in love. It was given as a tool to help not to harm.

WHO IS IN THE ROOM? THE HOLY SPIRIT, ANGELS, AND DEMONS

Feeling the powerful, unexplainable presence of God through the precious Holy Spirit is my favorite thing to experience in this entire world. Our Father never intended for us to *only* know Him by the Bible, but by His Spirit, His, presence, and His power. In deliverance ministry, it is helpful to discern the presence of the Holy Spirit, angels, and demons. It is not necessary, but it is certainly valuable. There was a time when I would read books about people seeing and feeling the presence of angels, and I began to ask the Father to show me the difference between the Holy Spirit, angels, and demons, because I was not sure how to tell them apart. I had learned to distinguish the presence of the Holy Spirit from early on in my walk, but I didn't think I knew the presence of angels and demons. The thing is, the Lord had shown me. I had just not fully processed the difference.

I will attempt to explain how you can tell one from the other, but because the presence of the Holy Spirit and God's angels may feel slightly different to everyone, I ask that you not put God in a box. The Holy Spirit's presence is most often felt in any of the following ways or in combination them: warm, hot, healing, like a burning fire, heavy, joyful, literal goosebumps, endless laughter, a sleepy feeling over your eyes, weeping, falling over in any direction because His glory is heavy, electricity, or inability to move. However, fear is not as common with His presence. Initial fear may arise, because we don't understand what is happening, but it does not linger.

God's angels lightly descend upon you. I have never seen an angel while I was awake as many have, but I have certainly felt their presence which feels like a light pressure and air coming down, with a slight warmth. I have seen angels in dreams. They have often looked human, but giant-sized. Fallen angels, also known as demons, also appear in the same fashion, but their presence will cause a feeling of anxiety that begins to rise on the inside and may make you feel sick to your stomach. When I have felt their presence descend on several occasions, I have commanded them to leave. If they ever present themselves to you in your sleep, you will know, because you may become physically paralyzed, fear may overtake you, and you may detect a drastic drop in room temperature. Just because you are sleeping does not mean you have to put up with their *visits*. Once you figure out that they are demonic, you begin to resist them even in your sleep.

Knowing that God has His Holy Spirit and His angels with you provides an assurance that His assignments are being fulfilled and that He takes pleasure in the work that is taking place.

STORIES WITH TRAINING PRINCIPLES

THE FOLLOWING ARE stories based on true events that I have been a part of, and I unapologetically share them, because so many individuals want to know they are not alone. If you or someone you have been working with has been made to feel hopeless, today is a new day! I am going to include a compilation of stories which will be based on truth; however, I will change certain details, such as names and situations, to protect identities, even though they have given me permission to freely share. As you read the stories, be sure to look for the training principles included.

These stories are not shared for the sake of putting out a good narrative, or to give you the chills, but rather to train and activate you as minister and/or recipient of the deliverance of the Lord. Some stories reveal various levels of demonization and freedom. All are equally as important. You will find yourself activated and more aware of any need for deliverance for yourself and others. I have included a story with every form of freedom ministry technique mentioned throughout the book.

People can be released while reading these stories, because the truth sets us free. I will be including simple prayers and declarations of blessing, freedom, and deliverance to help further the process for you and those you minister to in the future.

AN ITEM THAT DIDN'T BELONG

A friend and I visited a home and we began to take an inventory of items that were inviting unwanted guests. Before we agreed to visit the owner's home, she had been feeling as if something was not right. Once we began to explore, we found there was plenty that needed to be disposed of, as she was unaware of their effects. Items such as candles for specific use were present, but one particular item really made an impression.

She had been holding on to a book that someone gave her. It was a book based on a dark religion that promotes violence as a requirement to be accepted by a god. When she brought the book out and sat it next to me, I instantly began to feel a dark presence descend, and I began to feel sick to my stomach with a surge of anxiety and heaviness over my body, especially my arms.

As soon as I realized that the book was the culprit, I took it out of her home and disposed of it so that no one would find it and experience the same issue. We had her renounce ever bringing any of those items into her home. She didn't realize what she was storing until she saw the effects that day. Of course, some people bring in items willingly, but we say to them, "If you want full liberty, discern and dispose."

I try to keep my home clean of anything that represents idols, drugs, alcohol, sex, death, witchcraft in any form, and items that represent other religions. This is not the entire list as I simply utilize discernment, and if something is questionable, I ask the Lord. There are times when we may make an exception on something and realize later that the item should have never made it into the home. Don't condemn yourself if that has happened to you. Simply break up with the item by renouncing it and be on alert in the future.

BLESS AND DO NOT CURSE

I was ministering to a young person who we will call Abby. Abby had someone in her life since childhood that absolutely hated her very existence. This particular person loathed the relationship Abby had with a third person (a family member), which connected all three of them. This young woman had been bullied with words of death over her for many years. With no fault of her own, she was constantly spoken over with accusations and malicious words that release hate and bitterness, and these invoked evil over her.

As the years went by, she noticed depression, sadness, drugs, and a constant series of closed doors, with no advancement in her life. Abby felt her life was spinning out of control in so many different areas as well. After years of putting up with those kinds of results, she cried out to the Lord to set her free and change her circumstances.

Abby's life began to change shortly after we met and after we broke the word curses spoken over her life. During one of our visits, I felt the Holy Spirit boldly on the inside of me, and He directed me to bless her before doing anything else. I began to bless her, and immediately after speaking the blessing, I said, "In the Name of Jesus, I break every ungodly word that has been spoken over you. You will see your calling come to pass!" In addition, I spoke other words of blessing the Lord instructed me to say at that moment. Immediately, as I began to bless, and before I could even begin to break word curses, she became bold with a harsh breath, her face swelled a bit, and she was not completely present mentally (a manifestation).

Demons who had been assigned to make her life hell on earth were being uprooted by someone who knew truth and believed it on her behalf. This went on for a few minutes, then she was set free. A piece of advice I give those I see in a session who feel like they are losing control of their mind is to simply say the name of "Jesus," until they feel in full control again. The purpose of me telling them this is so that they will remain grounded in truth so that episode will quickly pass.

It was not long after our initial meeting that Abby began to live in joy and peace, and doors that had been closed for years, including opportunities to pursue what she knew God had put into her heart since she was a young girl, began to open. The exciting events that unfolded were beyond what she was expecting, including international expansion in her career. God is good!

Some individuals are so broken that they do not know any other way to do life, except to break others on the way. She happened to be a victim of that brokenness. However, the Lord heard her cry. If this has been your experience, and words of evil, abuse, bitterness, belittling, or other hurtful things have been spoken over you, let's get you free right now.

Prayer: In the Name of Jesus, I am blessed, favored, redeemed, loved, accepted, and chosen in Jesus Christ. I will accomplish what the Lord has set for me to accomplish. I break all word curse assignments, their power, effects, and false identities they have bound me with. I command all the works of evil against me, my past, my present, and my future to be broken now and for good, in Jesus' Name, Amen.

You can repeat this prayer if you felt a physical reaction or resistance of some sort or until you feel fully freed. I can tell you that words spoken over us are like chains of torment and barricades between us and our future, our prosperity, health, good relationships, and much more. Unbelievably, when we walk around with demonic activity as a cloud and torment, it causes others to reject us, without us or them even knowing why.

Some will say, "I am highly favored, and no devil can stop that!" I say, "Amen to that!" Faith, a well-established identity in Christ, and determination to see God's goodness manifest over your life will leave no room for darkness to play a part, but not everyone has that faith or understanding of how this works. So, for those who are learning who they are in Christ, this prayer will help speed up the journey!

Did you notice I did not instruct you to return the curses to the sender? Some ministers pray to return the word curses to the sender. I believe they intend to send it back to the *demonic* enemy that caused the torment to begin with. I do not want to take a chance at sounding like I would curse a human being, so for me, I break the curses, bless the individuals, and allow God to be the vindicator and the One who will bring justice! If I ever do return the curse to the sender, it is always to the enemy himself.

A SPIRT OF ANGER GETS EVICTED

There had been much activity surrounding a young woman we will call Olivia. This woman had been through deliverance before at different seasons in her life. However, there was one lingering devil that I knew had not been evicted by her prior deliverance sessions months before. I picked up a friend and said, "We're going to Olivia's home and getting her free."

As I was driving to Olivia's home, the Holy Spirit put a heavy burden in my heart for her. I began to pray in tongues and the Holy Spirit began rebuking this demon. I was able to interpret some of what He was saying through me. At that time, I did not know what was going to show up. Always expect the unexpected. We got to her home and were met with a bad attitude and some resistance from Olivia, but I knew she did not understand why. I confronted her about some things and asked if she wanted to be free. When she said yes, I felt the boldness of the Holy Spirit rise up. He then revealed the nature of that devil tormenting her, which was anger, and I began to command the demon of anger to leave her. My words were something like, "In the Name of Jesus I command you to leave now and never to return!"

Following the command, she went silent. Her tongue rolled up and she could not talk. I asked her a question and her arms and her legs lifted upward while she sat on a bench. All she could do was cry in silence as tears rolled down her cheeks. Most people would have thought they were watching the exorcist movie. As intense as this sounds, and it was, God still wins! That devil had to leave at the command in the name of Jesus. Not only was it an intense day, but also an emotional one, as she understood the depth of her bondage and the love God had for her, even in her state. From time to time, this process can seem to take longer than an instant expulsion. Keep going, and do not give in.

ALL TOGETHER NOW-CORPORATE DELIVERANCE

Years ago, I attended my first corporate deliverance meeting hosted by a ministry friend. Not long after this event, I took a trip to the Caribbean to minister and decided I would utilize the new learning I had acquired. While I was preaching, I took the attendees through deliverance. I simply said something to the effect of, "In the Name of Jesus I bind every demonic entity from you and cast them out! I command all generational devils to be loosed from you, witchcraft devils (which are common there), spirits of lust, depression, perversion, and suicide to be gone in Jesus' Name!"

One sure thing is that the Holy Spirit will tell you what is there. You just have to trust His voice. And when I do not know what is there, I simply say, "And I command all other entities unknown to me but known to God to leave now and never come back in Jesus' Name!" Freedom came for them. I had several testimonies from individuals who felt something happening in them and the deliverance they experienced.

I don't need to know every name of every entity that was there, just like I don't need to know every sin, to get people free. Let's activate faith in a greater capacity so that we can see salvation and freedom for many. In fact, I actually do not have to *say* anything for people to get free during a conference or preaching meeting. The Holy Spirit has full reign when I have the opportunity to speak and minister anywhere, which means He will be getting work done even without me! These are His meetings, so I ask Him to do what God wants. I love it when the Holy Spirit moves and the minister simply invites God's sweet and powerful presence.

HOLY SPIRIT FIRE OVER A WITCHCRAFT DEVIL

It was a powerful event. There was worship lead by an African team who had not scheduled restrictions on our time for worship. They worshipped and praised until the glory of God was so heavy, one could barely walk. Most everyone seemed to have an expectant heart for God's Spirit and power to manifest with healing and deliverance and so much more. And that is exactly what happened. The special guest preached a powerful word to stir the faith in the attendees. Soon after the preacher began to minister through the power of the Holy Spirit. This man did not have to lay hands on the individuals for God to touch them. God can do His work with and without the laying on of the hands.

He spoke and said to a woman, "I deliver you from the generational witchcraft devil from your family in Jesus' Name!" And, immediately the fire of God poured over her through the belly as you saw her fold over and receive her deliverance. She left the place set free and ready to pursue what God had for her. According to her, she did have witchcraft in her family. This was discernment at work in that man and a testimony that God set her free, no doubt!

AWAKENING

I was preaching a message based on Genesis 26 about uncovering the wells of blessing that the enemy would like to keep covered through our prior generations. After I shared that message, I gave an altar call for people to come to receive freedom if they believed they needed and wanted liberty. Most of the church came forth. As I spoke blessing over the congregation, I broke loose the unknown things covered up in their lives that the enemy was using to take from them their God-given rights.

As I prayed, I saw a young man shake his head as if he had been blinded or asleep and shaking it off. No intense manifestation, just healing, freedom, and deliverance. God has a gentle way of setting people free as well. Not everything is a demonic power encounter. And if it were, we won because Christ Jesus won! The commandment I stated was, "In Jesus' Name, I command all hidden things to come to the light and loose you now! Let all the bondage that resists your growth and freedom be broken!" If you learn to take the declaration and commandment principles I am sharing, you can help set anyone free from anything.

THE STORY OF A LITTLE MECHANICAL PIG

A man showed up to a Bible study one day. The congregants had never seen him before. They soon noticed the visitor quickly made himself at home, but something was off. The members noticed that if someone would share something he disagreed with, he would aggressively raise his voice and begin to rebuke and demand that everyone saw things as he did. This went on for weeks, and they all attempted to extend grace as they figured he just needed to be loved through the frustrations. The disrespect continued and simply shifted from one person to the next.

One day he attacked another person's comments which were being shared to help the group understand Scripture better. One of the leaders of that small group, Jordan, finally had enough and insisted that this man stop or leave if he could not stop being disrespectful. This only infuriated the visitor, and his abuse became aggressively directed toward Jordan. Eventually, this ended but not without resistance on the way out.

Within a day, the lead pastors received correspondence from this man demanding they get rid of Jordan, or something bad was going to happen to that church. That was his way of cursing this place. After that occasion, the Bible study group never saw him again, but that did not mean he stopped coming by. The following Sunday, he came by the church parking lot while someone was driving him. He sat in the back seat with his head lowered, and when he saw a church member going into the building, he called her to the car. He handed her an envelope and said, "Hand it to the leader that confronted me."

Of course, it was handed to Jordan, who was smart enough not to open the letter. The small group leader felt a presence in his home the next day, an upper-ranking demon. Jordan began to pray and command that all demonic presences leave, but there was such a resistance.

That evening, the leader's son went to bed, but

shortly after, he came out of his room and said he was afraid. He said he saw evil eyes on his computer screen staring at him. Although they were a family aware of spiritual warfare, they didn't really say much to the child because he was young and very sensitive, and they didn't want to cause him fear. Jordan explained to his wife what had happened earlier that day, and the resistance he felt. They both began to pray when suddenly their daughter in another room across the hall started screaming with fear. Jordan ran into her room and simply yelled out, "JESUS!" Then she suddenly stopped screaming and crying.

You see, as they prayed in their son's room and anointed it with oil, that demon stepped into her room and a mechanical piggy she had on the dresser started oinking and shaking really fast. The pig was off, and yet it was still moving and making noise. They knew that man *invoked* evil from the depths of his heart. After that day, all the drama ceased, and life continued for this family as usual.

SPIDERS ON MY LEGS

There was a man named Joe. Joe was being ministered to, and soul ties were an issue for him. As we broke soul ties from him regarding a large number of sexual partners, he experienced a bodily reaction more than once. There was one particular time that prompted a dramatic response from this man. Apparently, Joe had dated a witch. Although he did not actually partake in any of those practices, somehow, he still felt a connection with that woman.

When we broke the soul ties to that particular partner, he rose up and began to dust his legs off really fast. He felt lots of spiders on his legs, even though he would assure you that there was no such thing, even though it felt real. He got his freedom and for that we can praise the Lord!

THE MOCKING DEVIL

We met with a severely demonized woman. This woman manifested many different devils at different times, but one in particular really stands out—a mocking demon. To this day it bothers her a good bunch that this devil took so much pride in his mocking personality, but let's all rejoice that he was evicted to never return.

For whatever reason, whether to show off or try to scare everyone, he showed his personality and would mock at everything we would say. His response was, "Nope, nope, nope, nope!" Followed by a ridiculous laugh. When it was time for him to go, his angle became extremely frightened, begging to stay, and eventually, he was cast out. Devils may resist, but we must stand our ground and post in the authority of Christ.

HOLY SPIRIT TELLS YOU WHO IS THERE

Trusting the voice of the Holy Spirit can be developed by hearing it more than once and being willing to trust and obey what He says. He not only speaks, but He may also give you a visual to reveal information you and I need to know to get free and to bring freedom to others. During a freedom session, I stay in tune with the Holy Spirit so that I know what and where I need to target. In fact, I stay in tune with Him at all times, because I love to hear in my spirit, and audibly, what He has to say about any particular thing. This is necessary to live and experience what is referred to as the "Spirit-filled life."

Once you get used to hearing Him, He may tell you where in the flesh these things may be and the type of evil that is present, such as this passage, "And a woman was there who for eighteen years had been crippled by a spirit; she was bent over, completely incapable of standing erect" (Luke 13:11).

These conquered foes have functions and names just like Lucifer did. There are deliverance ministers that believe people cannot be free unless you ask them their names and command them to leave by that name. The woman was bent over, so it was apparent where this affliction was taking place and its function.

The Lord can still tell you where the affliction resides in a person if it is not clear by just looking at them. And, even if you don't know *exactly* who and what, freedom is still possible by simply commanding anything that is "unknown to you but known to God."

Following is a story to help get a mental picture of how the Holy Spirit speaks during a deliverance meeting.

A woman named Tara was dealing with severe frustration and rejection regarding her relationship with her mother, among other issues. During our ministry time, I began to minister to her based on what I felt was present. While she did carry with her the many issues she brought up, the Lord showed me a coil around her belly. When I spoke to the coil and released her from it, she began to vomit. The words that came out of my mouth were not complex. They were something like, "In the Name of Jesus I command that coil holding on, to let go now!" I didn't ask its name, I just knew it had a function and the oppression was in her belly. I would have never known that by my own imagination.

19

DOES EVERYONE STAY FREE?

I wish I could tell you that everyone stays free, but they don't. "Like a dog that returns to its vomit Is a fool who repeats his folly" (Proverbs 26:11). Removing demons is easy compared to renewing and changing people's minds, which is the key to staying free. I don't say that in arrogance, I simply mean that devils are not usually the reason people return to their previous state. It is the individual's flesh and carnal mind that puts them back to their previous state and worse than before.

Read the book of Romans, specifically chapters seven and eight. See how sin lives in the flesh and how we are not to empower it or live in bondage to its desires. However, like the Corinthian church that was saved but lived like the unsaved, nothing has changed today.

"For those who are according to the flesh set

their minds on the things of the flesh, but
those who are according to the Spirit, the
things of the Spirit. For the mind set on the
flesh is death, but the mind set on the Spirit
is life and peace, because the mind set on the
flesh is hostile toward God; for it does not
subject itself to the law of God, for it is not
even able to do so, and those who are in
the flesh cannot please God.
However, you are not in the flesh but in the
Spirit, if indeed the Spirit of God dwells in
you. But if anyone does not have the Spirit
of Christ, he does not belong to Him. If
Christ is in you, though the body is dead
because of sin, yet the spirit is alive because
of righteousness. But if the Spirit of Him
who raised Jesus from the dead dwells in
you, He who raised Christ Jesus from the
dead will also give life to your mortal
bodies through His Spirit who dwells
in you"

— ROMANS 8:5-11

Can you see how the mind, which does not submit to God's will, is at war with God? May that not be any longer, sweet believers in Christ. Let's submit to God, get free, and stay free!

"Submit therefore to God. Resist the devil and

he will flee from you. Draw near to God
and He will draw near to you. Cleanse your
hands, you sinners; and purify your hearts,
you double-minded"

— JAMES 4:7-8

This mind and our thinking include the company we entertain and how we spend our time. How do we expect to see change if we are not willing to do anything different? We watch the same shows, listen to the same music, talk the same way as when we were unsaved, hang out with the crowd, read the same books, and think the same thoughts instead of renewing our mind. Want to stay free? Knowing, believing, and applying God's Word will accomplish this for you and me. Let's not crucify Christ over and over again by giving ourselves over to the same chains that were once broken from us. Stay broken up with darkness.

20

GENTLE DELIVERANCE: PRAYERS, DECLARATIONS, AND PROCLAMATIONS

GENTLE DELIVERANCE IS a term I have coined to express a more tender approach in helping people renew their minds and live in freedom through prayers and declarations. The Lord, the heavens, the earth, angels, and demons know what I am declaring and releasing in these prayers without saying anything that gives the enemy too much attention. They *all* have a full understanding of what I call Freedom Language, another term I have coined, that keeps God magnified and the enemy where he belongs, under our feet.

Although this is a more tender approach, do not doubt it works. There is power behind it. You will sense freedom through these confessions, declarations, and prayers! We can never go wrong with praying, proclaiming, and declaring God's will over our lives. You may use these for yourself and others, but I encourage you to learn the principles and eventually learn to pray and follow the Holy Spirit's leading without needing to use these verbatim.

I will include several prayers dealing with specific things such as the Lordship of Jesus Christ in your life, hearing God's voice, joy, a healthy body, a sound mind, rejection, and others. I have addressed these specifically because these are the most common themes for those who visit with me.

Within these prayers, I am dealing with rebellion, jealousy, anger, rage, lust, witchcraft and the occult, soul ties, perversion, habits, and so much more, without focusing on giving darkness a platform through my words. In addition, I will include a general thorough prayer of declarations and proclamations that will address many other issues in one. Remember, the focus is on identity while attacking the darkness behind it.

DECLARATION OF THE POWER OF THE BLOOD OF JESUS: THE BLOOD COVENANT THAT DELIVERS

In the Name of Jesus, I pronounce a blessing over my life. My Father in heaven loves me. He sent His Son, Jesus Christ of Nazareth, to die on the cross and rise again with keys to death, hell, and the grave. His love is beyond extraordinary, and He provided the only blood sacrifice necessary for my freedom.

Jesus, I confess that Your blood has set me free, and it is the only sacrifice necessary for me to be in right standing with You. I dedicate my spirit, heart, mind, emotions, will, body, and my all to be indwelled by You through Your Holy Spirit. In Jesus' Amen!

Confession that God Speaks and I hear God's Voice

God, because I belong to You, I can hear Your voice as Your Word says. You reveal Your thoughts to me by the power of Your Holy Spirit who indwells in me. I reject all the lies that say You do not speak to me and that say I cannot hear You. Speak, Lord, I am listening. Heighten my sensitivity to hear Your voice. Give me a heart of obedience toward what You reveal in me. I separate myself from traditions and false teachings that say You no longer speak. You continuously speak to me as a loving Father does. I am listening, my God, speak. Amen.

Confessing that I Have a Joy on the Inside of Me & Overcoming Depression and Despair

I have a joy that exudes within me that belongs to the One who gave me the power to overcome sadness, depression, despair, and anxiety. It was a free gift paid for with the blood of Christ, and it is the medicine I need for my body, soul, mind, and spirit. There is none like it.

I am overcome by this joy, and it has overtaken darkness that has rested like a cloud. I separate myself from the overbearing net. I have been given life in abundance, and I will make the best of it until the end of my God-ordained days! The Lord fills me with a healing laughter. In Jesus' Name!

Confession that My Body is a Temple of Righteousness

My body brings glory to God. It is used for works of righteousness which are right in God's sight. I no longer desire to use my body and any part created by God Himself for sin, darkness, and unclean acts that pervert my soul and my body and defile my spirit. God, You are Healer and Deliverer. Therefore, I dedicate my body to you. Let all other agreements I made by my actions with my body, mind, soul, and spirit be canceled. In Jesus' Name, Amen.

My Affections and Worship Belong to Jesus

Jesus, my affections and worship belong to You alone. You are the only One worthy to be praised, and all my practices of adoration are toward You. Let anything that would want to take Your place in my life be removed in the Mighty name of Jesus!

When I said yes to Jesus, I said no to anything else that ever had my soul, my future, my past, my present, my commitment, and my attention. Jesus, Your blood sacrifice and covenant for me replaced all other false and dark practices in my life. In Jesus' Name, let the truth of this freedom be fully established now.

CONFESSION OF THE SOUND MIND OF CHRIST

My mind is one with the Lord Jesus Christ. It is calm, aware, sane, and in line with what God wants for me. Confusion is gone, and clarity of mind is mine. I proclaim the wholeness of the Lord Jesus Christ in me. The right and manifestation of the sound mind belongs to me and my family members before and after me. I decree that our minds are full of power and love. The net of confusion no longer rules! In Jesus' Name, Amen!

DECLARATION OF GOD'S SUCCESS OVER MY LIFE

I have a blood-bought right to the abundant life, and today I command it to manifest. The Lord has declared His blessings and destinations over me. The purpose He created me for will unveil before my eyes, and nothing can hide, deny, or resist that. I find the opportunities, relationships, and connections orchestrated for me before I was formed in the womb.

The barriers that were once walls between me and my destiny are removed today by the power of the Lord Jesus Christ. I separate myself, and today I stop agreeing with darkness regarding my future, health, marriage, prosperity, my children, career, ministry, and all that is attached to my name as long as I live. In Jesus' Name, Amen.

ACCEPTANCE IN CHRIST

I am accepted in the Beloved, and nobody's rejection or abandonment in my life can be greater than Christ's acceptance. Through the sacrifice of the cross and resurrection of the Lord Jesus, the way was made for me to enter into peace with my Father in heaven. I renounce the entities connected to and the effects of rejection and abandonment that have claimed the joy and blessing over my life. I am God's child, not an orphan. He is the Father to those who are or feel fatherless. His love reaches the broken portions of my mind, will, emotions, spirit, body, and life as it releases healing. I receive God's acceptance of me. I loose myself from the effects of rejection, even from the time I was being formed in the womb to my present day. In Jesus' Name, Amen!

HEALING FOR THE MIND, WILL, AND EMOTIONS & BECOMING FREE FROM TRAUMA

Father, I thank you that Your healing is a balm upon my soul (mind, will, and emotions). I welcome and receive restoration upon anything that is afflicted or broken in me because of past traumas, hurts, abuse, disappointments, and life's events. I command anything attached to the memories of (name the trauma, abuse or hurts) be released now. I separate myself from the effects of brokenness and receive wholeness, healing, truth, and restoration, in Jesus' Name, Amen!

FORGIVENESS FOR MYSELF AND OTHERS

In the Name of Jesus, I forgive myself for the activities, failures, abuses, and all ungodly actions I participated in, allowed, and willingly gave myself to. I release myself from the binds of guilt, shame, condemnation, and their effects that torment me. I disown the voices of accusation, and I receive the truth of forgiveness that Jesus provided for me. I am free! I choose to forgive those who have participated in the ungodly choices with me. I bless their lives and release myself from them and from any tie that binds us together. I will not mock the cross with unforgiveness toward myself or others. In Jesus' Name, let them be released! Amen.

SETTING MYSELF FREE FROM TIES TO UNHEALTHY PEOPLE AND RELATIONSHIPS

Father, in Jesus' Name, I break every ungodly soul tie that I formed with anyone, knowingly and unknowingly. Let every effect of darkness created through my connection with others in my past be broken now. I release myself from the things that will not willingly bow their knee to Jesus Christ, the Lamb of God. Amen.

GENERAL PRAYER

Father in heaven, in Your Son's Name, I submit myself to You. Let all my affections, worship, and adoration be solely for You. There is nothing that I have ever given myself over to that can take Your place today. I separate myself from and renounce all the works of the flesh, including commitment to the occult and witchcraft of any sort, perverted sexual behaviors, sexual acts against me by anyone in my life, the bondage of my emotions including anger, rage, jealousy, fear, and addictions that attempt to take Your place. I command all attacks on my identity in You to flee.

Cycles of familial sin, poverty, delay of purposes and callings, rebellion of the heart toward You, and traditions of men I have knowingly and unknowing subscribed to that make Your Word of no effect, cultural traditions that overlook the truth in the Bible, and loyalty to people and culture, rather than to You. I break and disown them all now, in Jesus' Name!

I separate myself from and renounce all ungodly ties that I have formed with people due to my sexual activity or ungodly emotional connections that I formed knowingly and unknowingly. Let all that torments me because of these past and present activities be released from me now, In Jesus' Name. Father, let truth prevail and begin to penetrate, saturate, and infiltrate my soul, mind, will, body, and emotions with godliness.

Let all other issues that are unknown to me but known to You, be considered in this confessional and renunciation. I give my will over to You so that you may mold it according to Your desires. I will take up my cross from now on and begin to live a life of godliness. Let freedom reign today, In Jesus' Name! Amen.

As I said before, I want freedom to be simple for you

and others. This is a great way to begin to experience what was already paid for at the cross and resurrection. Any of those prayers can be used for other needs. You can replace the wording with any situation and add it to these prayers if that helps. I trust that you have experienced a sense of freedom today!

21

THE PSALM THAT BREAKS FORTH FREEDOM

THE FOLLOWING prayer is based on Psalm 18. It is one of the most powerful freedom and deliverance Psalms. I have edited the prayer quite a bit to fit your name or someone else's. There are other amazing Psalms, but I thoroughly enjoy this one and have been using as needed for years now. This is a Psalm I use when there is an intense need for freedom, but it does not mean you cannot use it at any time. I have added parentheses where you would need to add your name or the name of the person to whom you are ministering to at the time. If I feel it is necessary, I read it out loud.

In Jesus Name, (we/I) cut the cords that encompass (name) and the torrents that terrify her/him/me within her/his/my soul, flesh, and spirit.

May the cords of Sheol surrounding (name) be severed in Jesus Name.

May the snares of death be confronted and dismantled from (name) now in the name of Jesus.

We call upon the name of the Lord!

(We/I) adjure a shaking of the earth upon the enemies working against (name), and may the foundations of evil shake, quake, and tremble, causing them to be demolished now in Jesus' Name.

Lord, release smoke from your nostrils and fire from your mouth to kindle coals that will devour, destroy, and loose the enemies against (name) from within or without, including all they have planned for your child.

Mighty God, utter thunder, hailstones, and coals of fire within the soul, flesh, and spirit of (name).

Hurl your arrows and scatter them, and let your abundant lightening rout the demons to the feet of Jesus that He may deal with them according to their evil schemes.

Sanction your channels of water to overtake the workings against (name). Draw her/him/me out of the many waters set up within, around, and without her/him/me by these entities. Cause the waters to betide these enemies.

The Lord delivers (name) from the strong enemy, even from those too mighty for her/him/me.

The enemies causing calamity in (name) are confronted today, and the Lord supports, protects, and sustains her/him/me.

The Lord is bringing forth (name) into freedom because He delights in (name).

Today the Lord is rewarding (name) according to

his/her/my righteousness. (Name) is the righteousness of God in Christ Jesus.

Because of the sacrifice of blood that Jesus provided on the cross for (name), she/he is free!

The Lord has saved (name) from her/his affliction today while abasing their enemies.

For Your Holy Spirit lights up her/his spirit and illuminates her/his path.

By You, (name) runs upon a troop and leaps over walls.

Your way is blameless, and Your Word is tried. It works, it is effective, sharper than any two-edged sword. May it divide to the very flesh, soul-mind, will, emotions, and spirit, uprooting the work of the enemy and yet providing a canopy and a shield upon, around, and within (name).

For there is no other God but the Lord! There is no one more powerful as the Rock, our God. God encircle (name) with a supernatural ring of strength.

We proclaim upon the feet of (name), feet like a deer's feet, immovable, unshakeable, able to jump through the traps of the enemy and ahead of the enemy. We proclaim upon (name) to sit upon high and exalted places the Lord has set for (name).

We loose upon (name) wisdom, understanding, and a God-given knowledge that prepares and trains her/him for this battle. Her/his arms will bend a bow of bronze and shoot it upon her/his enemies today.

Your salvation is her/his/my shield, and she/he/I take(s) hold of it as a piece of armor while the Lord's right hand upholds (name) and His gentleness causes her/him/me to increase and excel in authority over her/his/my enemies.

Lord, thank You for making room for her/him/me to walk in freedom and for her/his/my feet not to slip and be a victim of the enemy traps set up for her/him/me.

In Jesus' Name, today she/he/I pursue(s) her/his/my enemies and overtakes them with no turning back until they are utterly consumed by the fire of God.

In Jesus' Name, shatter our enemies so they are never again able to rise. They fall under her/his/my feet by the authority they/I have in Jesus Christ of Nazareth.

(Name) is girded with strength, so we pray that she/he/I may be aware of the strength the Lord has put upon (name). Those demonic enemies against (name) are subdued today, and their backs are turned to her/him/me with fear because they are to be destroyed today in Jesus' Name.

There will be no help or mercy for them. They shall be beat as fine dust before the wind and emptied out as the mud, as the swamps of the street.

The Lord delivers (name) from the contentions of her/his/my enemies making her/him/me captain and chief of all good things including his/her/my freedom, calling, and ministry.

As soon as the enemies without, around, and upon (name) hear her/his/my orders, they shall obey (name) and come trembling out of their fortresses and to the feet of Jesus that He may deal with them according to their wickedness.

The Lord lives, and blessed be our rock. Exalted be the God, her/his/my salvation, the God who executes vengeance for (name) and subdues enemies under them. He delivers (name) from his/her/my enemies. Surely You lift (name) above those who rise up against them. You rescue them from the violent man.

Therefore, we give thanks to You among the nations, O Lord, and we will sing praises to Your name. You give great deliverance to Your child (name) And show loving-kindness to Your anointed, to (name) and their descendants forever.

22

STARTING A FREEDOM AND DELIVERANCE MINISTRY

ARE you curious about starting a freedom and deliverance ministry? Maybe you don't want to start an official deliverance ministry where you spend several days a week in a location and people come to you, but you would like to begin to be obedient to the call of Mark 16. How would you start? Well, now that you are aware that God has given us the responsibility to set the captive free, you may begin to naturally run into people who need liberty.

You have already been around these individuals, no doubt, but you are now going to be aware when things are off. Of course, not every single person you meet will be a candidate, but many will. Regardless of whether you are active in this ministry or not, praying with others daily, or just want to start, there are some things I want to share that will be most important and prepare you to deal with yourself and with people.

COMPASSION

Compassion drove Jesus to heal and deliver. As a Christian and a minister, we must allow compassion to be our driving force. God had compassion on His creation, which is why we now have Jesus as our Mediator. This is not the time for us to hang a demon slayer sign on the door and to be overtaken by pride, although it happens. In many circles and churches, deliverance has become the new reality show, and everyone on social media is watching. This is a sure sign that the focus has been lost, and people have been taken away by a false feeling of power.

We are dealing with people's lives, so handle them carefully and lovingly. Don't deny them what Christ freely gave to you and me. If you lack in this area, start praying to become an effective, compassion-bound, grace-filled minister. That is the Lord's way of healing. Even if you don't think you are lacking compassion, pray anyway.

SANCTIFICATION

I have witnessed God use individuals who have sin in their life to set others free. I know this is hard to hear. Yet, it happens. Why? Because once again, He wants people free. However, I have also seen people endure such confusion, because believers want to work for and represent Christ and still live like the world. I am not only talking about the sins we would consider as really bad. I am talking about simple day-to-day habits that people live their lives by.

If we belong to Jesus Christ, we will purify ourselves and set ourselves apart (sanctify) in how we speak and the words we use, how we think, how we act, what we participate in, what we watch, what we support, and what we give ourselves to. Represent Him well. He deserves it! Pray the Lord shows you if there is anything that needs to be set upright in your life today, and be willing to break yourself from the rebellion that doesn't want to let go!

HUMILITY

When I meet a humble person, I really want to get to know them, and my respect level for them is typically immediate. It is not unlikely to meet someone in any area of ministry that could use a dose of humility. There are times when we may not even realize we need to humble ourselves. I pray for this often. It is not hard to forget where our strength comes from. Therefore, I encourage you to pray for this regardless if you feel you are well-founded in humility or not.

CONFIDENTIALITY

Working with broken individuals, you will be exposed to the most horrific, unclean details in the lives of others. If God or life does not train you to have a strong sense of confidentiality, you may one day use the details you hear to tickle someone else's ear. If the Lord trusts us with His children's secrets, that means we are not to share what they say in private. Even as I wrote this book, I would not disclose full details. Several people said, "Use and share anything you want about me because it will help someone else." I appreciated that greatly, but my conscience still says, "That is not wise."

Protect others' business and integrity. Shame has bound many for their past and present shortcomings. I never want to partner with the enemy by smearing that person's life along with him. Keep these details and information to yourself. This too must be prayed about, because it is a basic requirement for serving in any type of ministry.

PRAYER: A NORMAL AND DAILY OCCURRENCE

One way to begin to practice freedom ministry is to apply all the above foundations, including this one. I pray for anyone at any time. I practice it whether in person, at church, on the street, in my counseling, over the phone, or when I run into people. Ask the Holy Spirit to train you on how to approach and pray liberty for people. Many pray, and that is great, but they do not add the freedom focus, which includes being aware that the Holy Spirit wants to set people free. Those who meet you will appreciate you being intentional.

Since I first became a Christian, deeply broken people have gravitated toward me, even when I was still quite messed up and needed freedom and mind renewal myself. Yet, the Lord was not waiting for me to be perfect before He began to use me. These people would come into my life, and I would disciple them, and in time, also set them free. Invest in people. Let them find you trustworthy enough to pray for them about the darkest places in their lives. Let them know you care. They will ask for your help, trust me.

Every person we pray for is a divine appointment. The Lord will bring people into your life because there is more work than workers. Through pastoral counseling, and in my preaching, I am able to meet many who need help, but I also find people through my inner circles. Pray, "Lord prepare me, send me, use me."

What Deliverance Sessions Looks Like

Being that I offer pastoral counseling and deliverance ministry to the public, every one of my sessions has a similar foundation but can differ. If someone is looking for more of a pastoral visit, and they do not understand what I do, I take a slightly different approach. These people usually have little to no understanding of the Bible, oppression, or anything of that nature. Since they are looking for pastoral counseling, I will advise them on their life's issues according to the Word of God. I will assign Bible reading and meditating on what they read along with other basic homework assignments, because that is why they came to see me.

At the end of each session, I utilize the gentle deliverance approach, because it helps build their faith to hear words of power. After they practice this out loud, I will close the session with a prayer over them as I am led by the Holy Spirit. If I visit with them more than once, I continue to provide what they asked for, but I move closer to the deliverance and freedom approach. Truth sets people free. So, whether I am doing pastoral or more deliverance ministry, they will find freedom. Most of the time, I offer a combination of both. More than anything, even if I attempt to respect some boundaries, I follow the leading of the Lord, as He is the true Counselor in the room.

23

FIERY ARROWS: WHEN ALL HELL BREAKS LOOSE

WITHIN ONE DAY of finishing the first manuscript of this book, all hell began to break loose against my family. There was a situation that presented itself which left my husband and I in shock, sad, angry, and warring in prayer as we became aware that the enemy of our soul had come to steal, kill, and destroy, as the Word of God says.

The day after this unexpected attack, I headed to the location necessary to deal with rest of this unfinished business that we were now left to deal with. As I drove, I began to war in the Spirit (tongues) when righteous anger rose up in me. Suddenly, the Holy Spirit prompted me to write a chapter addressing the fiery arrows against the children of God as mentioned in Ephesians 6.

In reality, I should have written this section *before* this event even occurred. However, God is good, and this situation spurred me on to equip the believer with the truth and tools they need to come against larger scale demonic attacks that are launched from the outside and often affect every area of our lives, including the people we love.

These types of spiritual assaults often produce pain, hurt, anger, loss of time and money, shaky relationships, and several other issues. I am not sure anything will ever fully prepare us when shaky developments occur except an active faith. Even when I got the call regarding this storm, I could feel a rise of concern, but my heart stayed still. The Holy Spirit clearly said, "It is going to be OK," yet without His voice, it would have been easy to lose my composure. It is amazing that the Lord can assure you it is going to be OK while you stare at major chaos in the face. Even with God's assurance, the next few days felt like a roller coaster of feelings, thoughts, and uncertainties. We warred in prayer, wept, mourned, and did our best to pull close as a family.

After this event, I put the book down for a while *once again*. It has been edited and written in seasons which has helped me compose a much more transparent experience. Writing this type of material, and being in ministry in general, will get the attention of the enemy of our soul. All he needs is a willing participant which he can often find within our family, friends, money, health, etc., to launch the fiery darts. Since we have endured the pain of spiritual attacks, I am happy to share their purpose so that as you enter into this type of ministry, you are prepared and know that you will not be alone.

INITIAL REACTIONS

Flaming or fiery arrows are what the enemy releases against the children of God, according to Ephesians 6:16. When he releases them into our lives, through people and circumstances, they are kindled with anger toward us and grief that will devastate, and they are packed with the assurance of causalities. Our response toward each individual event is often based on where we are in our faith, or according to the pressure other unexpected circumstances have already placed on us. Yet, there are some very common emotions we will all face, and unfortunately, that is the enemy's plan. Let's visit each one individually.

ANGER

I am a warrior at heart with a strong temperament, and my first reaction to anything that stirs up my world is *anger*. This is the response most will have to anything that poses a danger to their family and life in general. The goal is to keep it under the *righteous anger* boundaries, of course. The Lord utilizes this emotion to catapult us into our position as prayer warriors and commanding the works of the enemy to flee from us and those we love. Let the war be righteous, and stand in truth, or the anger will become bitterness, which can block us spiritually.

My husband shared with me that on his way to tend to the situation at hand, he was so angry, praying and saying out loud, "Devil, you are going to pay for it!" He said the Lord reminded him, "Vengeance is mine." So, while we are justified for the pain Satan caused, the Lord is the One who will vindicate us. For a prayer of encouragement during difficult times, the entire chapter of Psalm 91 is powerful, although I have solely focused on the first five verses to use as a declaration in the midst of an attack over you or those you love.

Declaration: My family and I dwell in the shelter of the Most High, and we abide in the shadow of the Almightily. Lord, You are our refuge and fortress. We trust in You. You deliver us from the snare of the fowler and deadly pestilence. You cover us with your pinions and under Your wings we find refuge. Your faithfulness is a shield and buckler. We will not fear the terror of the night or the arrows that fly by day (Psalm 91:1-5).

PAIN AND HURT

The second common reaction to an attack is pain and hurt for you and those involved. This is both a normal part of the process when the unseen comes against us and it is also the intention of the enemy toward our lives. Pain is intended to make us lose hope, as it is the greatest form of involuntary vulnerability.

Have you ever noticed that many find it easy to get really close to the Lord when they are hurting, and then once they are back on their feet, they forget He was there? When we are vulnerable, we remove the barriers we hold up daily that keep these types of flaming arrows from hitting so hard. Yet, when we are hurting or see those we love are in pain, anything can pierce through quickly. We put down the shield of faith as we hurt and begin to feel hopeless immediately after the piercings of agony begin. This is common, and we have all been there. At times, it may be necessary to process the pain for a moment, then go back to our righteous anger stance.

When you read the following Scriptures, you will see that the Christian's *defensive* position must be held. There is no room for compromise.

> *"Finally, be strong in the Lord and in the strength of His might. Put on the full armour of God, so that you will be able to stand firm against the schemes of the devil. For our struggle is not against flesh and blood, but against the rulers, against the powers, against the world forces of this darkness, against the spiritual forces of wickedness in the heavenly places. Therefore, take up the full armour of God, so that you will be able to resist in the evil day, and having done everything, to stand firm. Stand firm therefore,* HAVING GIRDED YOUR LOINS WITH TRUTH, *and* HAVING PUT ON THE BREASTPLATE OF RIGHTEOUSNESS, *and having shod* YOUR FEET WITH THE PREPARATION OF THE GOSPEL OF PEACE; *in addition to all, taking up the shield of faith with which you will be*

*able to extinguish all the flaming arrows
of the evil one. And take* THE HELMET OF
SALVATION, *and the sword of the Spirit,
which is the word of God. With all prayer
and petition pray at all times in the Spirit,
and with this in view, be on the alert with
all perseverance and petition for all the
saints"*

— EPHESIANS 6:10-18

"Be strong!" "Put on!" "Take up!" "Stand firm!" "Extinguish all!" No settling! While I have experienced the hurt of the day of evil against my family and I, the option is to stand. Yes, we may cry, ask others to pray for and with us, but the decision to be immoveable comes from the will, the heart, and the spirit.

Some of you who will read this have been through some of the most horrific situations and may feel like you have done all the standing you can do. That is when you ask your friends to be the ones who hold you up until you regain your strength. If you don't have that kind of support, pray them in. I have prayed for friends, strong ones who know how to pray, who are faithful, trustworthy, graceful, and honest. The Lord has provided.

DISAPPOINTMENT

Disappointment can cause us to quit, and it is a

vicious and effective technique. I have seen the enemy use this tactic over and again. While we can still endure with hurt and anger, disappointment quickly opens the door to stagnation, resistance to advancement of any kind, and eventually to quitting. When we see what appears to be the enemy *winning* or evil always advancing against what we have been believing and standing for or warring against, it is easy to become embittered and think, "What's the point of going forward?" "Why keep doing this?" "What is the purpose if I am not seeing victory?"

While not everything works out the way we hope, the Lord brings forth something good, regardless of the outcome. I am being honest, because I know that not everyone has the ending they hoped for. However, I also know that we should never withdraw from our position of standing. If we sat down to create a list of the things the Lord has delivered into our hands, I would bet they would outweigh the negatives, and the answered prayers would be endless. Break off that spirit of disappointment. Don't allow it to claim your life, call, and purpose.

DEPRESSION

I have been through a short-term circumstantial depression more than once, as many of you have. Even though I stood, warred, and did all the things I knew to do, I still hit a hard emotional state. There were emotions and challenges I had to overcome. This is common for most of us. It took about two weeks to recover from the natural consequence of someone else's actions, plus the spiritual effects. We did rise again and are continuing to do so daily. People who love us stood up for us in prayer.

We cannot overcome everything alone. Remember that these seasons *will* end, even when they are long in duration. Our option is to overcome, as is yours. That is my determination in any instance, no matter how painful.

My last words regarding depression are that you must trust someone, or the isolation we tend to create when we are depressed will only make things worse. It doesn't hurt to get wise counsel if the situation requires an outside biblical perspective. In the meantime, I have included a declaration if you or someone you know is in a state of depression.

Declaration: In Jesus' Name, I command the web of depression and disappointment to be dismantled by the power of the Holy Spirit! I break myself and (name your family, friends, etc.) from this and any other demonic attachment that would like to bring forth the enemy's plan. I assert the plans and purposes of Jesus over our lives! In Jesus' Name!

I have reworded a Scripture to use as a prayer as well:

No weapon formed against (me/them) will prosper; And every tongue [and action] that accuses (me/them) in judgment Lord, You will condemn. This is the heritage of the servants of the LORD, and (my/their) vindication is from the Lord. (This is based on Isaiah 54:14.)

Fear of Criticism

How many of us have been concerned about what others think about us for too long? God forbid the attacks are with our children, because we will want to crawl under a table. Or, what about when it's the spouse, and the *secret* regarding their habit is out? And, I have an even better one. What about when we are active in ministry, filling leadership positions and helping roles such as pastors, ministers, counsellors, teachers, etc.? Aren't we expected to not have hell break out in our lives?

The enemy accuses individuals in serving roles more than anything, because people already have an expectation of them, so why not jump on board. I can say I have personally felt this before. When I sense it coming on, I immediately cast it off, because I recognize where that comes from. We must be free from this, or it will hinder our stance. If we have an expectation that those in our family need to walk a straight line or else someone may talk, we will eventually lose control of that false expectation.

Declaration: Through the new covenant blessing, my faith pleases God and not people. My acceptance comes from the Lord. His thoughts toward me determine what I believe about myself and those I love, and not my circumstances or the choices others make. I release myself from the worry and fear when situations arise. I renounce the desire to be approved by people and I exchange them for the truth that the Lord is pleased with me. In Jesus' Name, Amen.

FEAR OF THE FUTURE

Finally, the attacks may produce fear of the future. "Will this happen again?" "What if I cannot change this?" "Can I trust them now?" "Who will support me?" These are just a few of the questions that can result after a demonic blow. If we entertain the effects of the attacks a bit much, the shield of faith will be surrendered and compromised. Pick it back up if that is you. Our future is not dependent on the answers to those questions, because we don't have knowledge of what is to come. The longer we stop to ask these questions and others, the more certain we can be that we have begun to disarm ourselves from the weapons the Lord has provided for us to walk in power and victory.

> *"Be anxious for nothing, but in everything*
> *by prayer and supplication with*
> *thanksgiving let your requests be made*
> *known to God. And the peace of God,*
> *which surpasses all comprehension,*
> *will guard your hearts and your minds*
> *in Christ Jesus"*

— PHILIPPIANS 4:6-7

Declaration: Lord, my future is in Your hands. I

choose not to be uneasy about the future and will remain in a state of divine peace the Holy Spirit provides for me. I declare to heaven and earth that my prayers and supplications are being heard, and the answers are on the way. I command my future to line up with the will of God. Anything concerning my life, my family, my health, wealth, opportunities, and relationships must now line up to heaven's orders. In Jesus' Name, Amen!

24

FINAL EXHORTATION AND BLESSING

WHILE I CANNOT SHARE every single detail about the experiences I have acquired, I have gladly and openly communicated what I have put to practice for the last several years. I never would have imagined that I would be doing what I get to do today. Several months, maybe even a year before I started operating in freedom and deliverance ministry, I had a dream. In this dream was a tall man, with a large stature, wearing a Hawaiian shirt, khaki pants, and white hair. This man was in a public laundry mat teaching me how to wash clothes.

I didn't know what that particular dream meant until months later. The washing of the clothes represented getting people saved, healed, delivered, and free. The man teaching me to wash the clothes was exactly the role he would play in my life. It came true. I did meet this man, and he did teach me to set people free. For that, I will always be grateful.

There was so much that I learned through this time. Some things challenged me and my theology, and in turn, I challenged what I learned, not only from this man, but also from others who are well versed in deliverance ministry.

Every trip I took to the bookstore was for material regarding deliverance. Along with the books, I watched endless videos and devoted myself to learning what I could. What I have written is where I have landed and come to a good place about what I believe and what the Bible says. While there is a great amount of information out there, I encourage you to always make sure your final decision is based on the Bible. We can make a theology based on things we hear repeatedly. That does not make it God's truth.

Not everyone will accept your beliefs about this topic with bells ringing. Some individuals may only agree with a portion of what you believe and think. It is a fine thing to agree to disagree with someone in *love*. I urge you not to argue with people. "If it is possible, as far as it depends on you, live at peace with everyone" (Romans 12:18). In the end, if you want to please God, you will not be able to please people all the time. When you know you walk in truth, you can stand firm even when it hurts. So, stand tall!

May your experiences, understanding, and knowledge expound unbelievable. And before I leave you with what I trust has been filled with hope, encouragement, empowerment, and equipping, I am including a prayer of blessing over you. I am always aware the blessing is based on the premise of love. Love is a blessing, and a blessing comes because of love. When I minister to people, I try to ensure to speak blessing over them, because the Bible says we have the power to bless and to curse (James 3:10).

If blessing you overrides the lifeless words that have been released into your life, and I know it does because God is greater, I am compelled to bless those before me who have suffered delay, pain, rejection, oppression, and other issues. It is my duty to release the power of God over you so that you may begin to be free and walk out the identity of Christ that has been deposited in you.

BLESSING UPON THE READER

Father, in the Name of Jesus, I bless and lift up in prayer the person reading this book at this particular moment. I thank You, Lord for dying on the cross for them, and love is what took You there. You drew them in as Yours. Father, You have been pursuing them from the beginning of their time. You desire a relationship that is deeper than words could express. God, I praise You for loving them so dearly that You desire and have purposed good things for their lives. No matter where they have been, they are able to rise with strength and victory because of who You are in them. God, I thank You for releasing them from everything that has halted, hindered, and delayed their spiritual growth and progress in days past.

Father, I pray they develop a mighty hunger for Your

Word, that they will never be able to fully satisfy it and will pursue it daily. I pray that they would desire to understand Your instructions and that revelation is released as they indulge in the Word that gives them life.

Father, I pray freedom for your people from wrong thinking that does not line up with Your truth. I thank You that their mind is being renewed as they read this prayer and declaration. You are a graceful God, and when we ask, You hear and do not leave us without answers. Thank you, Father, for lovingly shining the light on any situation that may be in their life that is not pleasing to You. I thank you that hidden things are revealed, and those which are done with intention are surrendered in Jesus' Name!

I command rebellion hiding these things in the dark to move out now and never return. They will no longer be in bondage to choices, behaviors, and lifestyles that are not in line with Your will, Jesus. Father, let your child grow in the things of You.

Father, I pray that You reveal Yourself to them as Father, Provider, Protector, Healer, Savior, Deliverer, and Lover of their soul. I thank you, my God, that You come in right now and heal the wounds in the heart and mind. Holy Spirit, minister to the embittered areas bound with pain and disappointment, and release them from that now in Jesus' Name! You, my God, will cause their faith to stir because faith comes by hearing, and they have heard truths. Let their hearts open up and begin to ask for more of You.

Lord reveal the things they do not understand, imagine, or comprehend. Holy Spirit, release a trust that You are supernatural God and You intended for us to experience You in a much deeper way. Teach them by experience and by Your Word what is true.

I pray that any traditions of man that make the Word of no effect be released from them. Let those lies that were taught and received that created resistance to who God is in the supernatural be loosed now in Jesus' Name! Let anything attempting to keep them from experiencing God through His Holy Spirit be removed.

I pray for those who want more of the Spirit-filled life, including the baptism of the Holy Spirit with speaking in tongues. Father, these are gifts You have freely given, and we do not have to beg or plead. Thank you for releasing to your children what their heart desires: more of You!

Holy Spirit, release the son or daughter from the doubts and barriers that may be attempting to block their spiritual advancement and experiences, attempting to keep them from their next level of growth. Thank you, my Lord, that You open up their minds to all that You want for them.

Lord, release an expansion for them now, to be released with humility, compassion, purity, and respect for the lives of others. Open their eyes, my God, to discernment, steadfastness, and wisdom. Let love for people expand and cause their hearts to break for those in bondage and in need of freedom. Father, let them see with spiritual eyes, that which is at work within those You have called them to deliver.

Fine tune their spiritual senses God, that they may know how to discern the presence of the Holy Spirit, angels, and the enemy. Speak loudly and clearly to them, my God, that they may be in tune with Your voice constantly. Speak to them in dreams and visions, and any other form that pleases You, my Lord.

Father let the boldness of the Holy Spirit swiftly rise up in them when facing darkness or danger for their own sake, and that of others. Let fear bow its knee in their presence, because they carry the very Holy Spirit, who raised Jesus from the dead, on the inside of them. Pierce their minds and hearts with the truth that You are pleased with them and that they can freely call you their heavenly Daddy, Abba Father! In the Mighty Name of Jesus I pray, Amen!

WORKS CITED

Ciuningham, Loren and David Hamilton. *Why Not Women?* YWAM Publishing, 2000.

Grady, Lee. *Ten Lies The Church Tells Women: How the Bible Has Been Misused to Keep Women in Spiritual Bondage*. n.d.

Vallotton, Kris. *Fashioned to Reign*. Chosen, 2013.

Zodhiates, Spiros, ed. *Key word Study Bible: New American Standard Version*.: The Lockman Foundation, 1995.

ABOUT THE AUTHOR

https://www.teresalusk.com

Through Spirit-led conferences and individual consultations, Teresa G. Lusk unapologetically empowers individuals to move beyond their past and present circumstances and into a better life through Jesus Christ. After triumphing over hurts of sexual abuse, teen parenting, dropping out of school in the 8th grade, participating in dark spiritual practices, and much more, Teresa passionately and unapologetically ministers with a determination for truth and freedom to others. In 1999, Teresa met Leon, and they married in 2001. Together they gave their hearts to Christ and were both saved and transformed. Teresa acquired an Associate of Arts in Business Administration and a Bachelor of Science in Multidisciplinary Studies, with an emphasis in Psychology, Religion, and Biblical Counseling. In addition, she earned a Masters in Professional Counseling.

The ministry entrusted to her is accomplished through submission to the fullness of the Holy Spirit through the gifts of the Spirit as listed in 1 Corinthians 12:8-10, and the commandment given in Mark 16:15-18.

Teresa is an ordained minister and offers pastoral counseling to the hurting community and has begun to extend the ministry to the Spanish speaking communities. Through social media outlets, and her television program called, FREEDOM TV with TERESA LUSK, Teresa ministers a transparent message of empowerment and deliverance and hosts special guests. Teresa is the founder of Teresa Lusk Ministries, a 501(c)(3) organization, and has written two books; Prayers that Change Us and Good Enough to be a Homemaker and CEO. Teresa's testimony has been aired on 100 Huntley Street and Full Circle.

Learn more at https://www.teresalusk.com

Made in the USA
Monee, IL
23 June 2023

36806507R00109